D0369209

The MIT Guide to Teaching Web Site Design

Digital Communication
Edward Barrett, editor

The Nurnberg Funnel: Designing Minimalist Instruction for Practical Computer Skill, John M. Carroll, 1990

Hypermedia and Literary Studies, edited by Paul Delany and George P. Landow, 1991

Rhetoric, Innovation, Technology: Case Studies of Technical Communication in Technology Transfers, Stephen Doheny-Farina, 1992

Sociomedia: Multimedia, Hypermedia, and the Social Construction of Knowledge, edited by Edward Barrett, 1992

The Digital Word: Text-Based Computing in the Humanities, edited by George P. Landow and Paul Delany, 1993

Contextual Media: Multimedia and Interpretation, edited by Edward Barrett and Marie Redmond, 1995

High Noon on the Electronic Frontier, Peter Ludlow, 1996

Forward through the Rearview Mirror: Reflections on and by Marshall McLuhan, edited by Paul Benedetti and Nancy DeHart, 1997

From Web to Workplace: Designing Open Hypermedia Systems, Kaj Grønbæk and Randall H. Trigg, 1999

Electric Rhetoric: Classical Rhetoric, Oralism, and a New Literacy, Kathleen E. Welch, 1999

Crypto Anarchy, Cyberstates, and Pirate Utopias, edited by Peter Ludlow, 2001

The MIT Guide to Teaching Web Site Design, Edward Barrett, Deborah A. Levinson, and Suzana Lisanti, 2001

The MIT Guide to Teaching Web Site Design

Edward Barrett
Deborah A. Levinson
Suzana Lisanti

The MIT Press
Cambridge, Massachusetts
London, England

This book was set in Sabon by The MIT Press.

Printed and bound in the United States of America.

Library of Congress Cataloging-in-Publication Data

Barrett, Edward.
  The MIT guide to teaching web site design / Edward Barrett, Deborah A. Levinson, Suzana Lisanti.
    p. cm. — (Digital communication)
  Includes index.
  ISBN 0-262-02500-0 (hc. : alk. paper)
  1. Web sites—Design—Study and teaching. I. Levinson, Deborah A. II. Lisanti, Suzana. III. Title. IV. Series.

TK5105.888 .B37 2001
005.2'76—dc21   00-066446

Trademark Information

Acrobat, Acrobat Reader, Illustrator, ImageReady, Photoshop, and Portable Document Format are registered trademarks of Adobe.

Apache is a registered trademark of Apache Software Foundation.

Macintosh, QuickTime, and QuickTime VR are registered trademarks of Apple Computer, Inc.

iPIX is a registered trademark of Internet Pictures Corporation.

Director, Flash, Freehand, and Shockwave are registered trademarks of Macromedia.

Internet Explorer, PowerPoint, Windows, and Windows Media are registered trademarks of Microsoft.

Netscape Communicator is a registered trademark of Netscape Communications Corporation.

QuarkXPress is a registered trademark of Quark, Inc.

Java is a registered trademark of Sun Microsystems.

RealAudio and RealVideo are registered trademarks of RealNetworks, Inc.

Unix is a registered trademark of X/Open Company, Ltd.

All other trademarks are the property of their respective owners.

Contents

Series Foreword   vii
Acknowledgments   ix
Introduction   xi
    Organization
    Design Philosophy

1   **Class Design and Curriculum**   1
    Why We Created This Class
    Why a Writing Class?
    Class Design and Curriculum
    Creating Your Syllabus
    The Proposal
    Class Web Site

2   **Team-Based Web Design**   17
    Team Size
    Why Identify Roles?
    Strategies to Facilitate Teamwork

3   **Planning a Web Site**   23
    Process Map

4   **Information Architecture and Designing Web Sites**   41
    Elements of Information Architecture
    Site Mapping
    Information Architecture and Graphic Design
    Graphic Design Fundamentals for the Web
    Grid
    Look and Feel

Typography
Color

5   **Servers, Security, Privacy, and Copyright   49**
Server Planning
Security and Encryption
Privacy
Intellectual Property

6   **Web Graphics   55**
Graphic File Formats
Adding Interactivity
Constraints

7   **Multimedia   65**
Alternative Text Formats
Sound, Video, and Beyond

8   **Programming for Interactivity   73**
Interactivity for Beginners
Intermediate and Advanced Interactivity
Caveats
Discussion Systems: An Object Lesson

9   **Testing and Evaluating a Web Site   81**
Interviews
Conduct a Series of Focus Groups
Gather Information from Available Logs
Conduct a Usability Test
Card Sorting
Survey a Wider Audience
Competitive Analysis
Analyze Your Data

10 **Case Studies   87**
Boston Chinatown: Finding the Look and Feel
SweatStats: Community and Interaction
Blitz: Portals—Vortals—Opinions

Afterword   99
Index   101

Series Foreword

Digital communication is one of the most exciting, rapidly expanding fields of study and practice throughout the world, as witnessed by the increasing number of Web sites and users of the Internet, as well as publication and use of multimedia CD-ROM titles in schools, homes, and corporate environments. In addition, Web and multimedia publications have created a vast secondary literature of scholarly analysis in a range of subject areas. Professional societies and degree-granting programs devoted to digital communication have steadily increased. And the language and concepts of digital life have become central in popular culture. In cyberspace the roles of writer and audience are no longer static but dynamic; the concept of text is no longer fixed but fluid. Computational technology has delivered us a powerful tool for the creation, presentation, exchange, and annotation of a text (in words, images, video, and audio)—so powerful that we speak in terms of transparent and seamless information environments that integrate all media.

We are witnessing a profound revolution in communication and learning in a post-Gutenberg world. The MIT Press series on Digital Communication will present advanced research into all aspects of this revolutionary change in our forms of expression, thought, and being. This research will be published in traditional book format or as Web sites or multimedia CD-ROM titles, as demanded by content. Whether this series finds its expression in hardcopy or in digital format, it will seek to explore and define new genres of thought and expression offered by digital media.

Edward Barrett

Acknowledgments

This guide reflects the experiences we have had working with students at MIT over the past six years. Perhaps our greatest debt of gratitude is to these talented students who have shared with us their desire to learn, their talents, and creative imaginations. We would also like to thank Professor James Paradis, Head of the Program in Writing and Humanistic Studies at MIT for his continuing and generous support for this class. A special thanks must also be given to Mr. Daniel S. Stevenson, now a graduate student at the Media Lab at MIT, for his collaboration throughout the years, both in classroom instruction and in the early stages of planning this guide book. The class has received invaluable contributions from several guest lecturers, including Karen Hersey, MIT Intellectual Property Counsel; Hagan and David Rivers, of Two Rivers Consulting; Joanne Costello, MIT's Information Systems; and Nicole Hennig, MIT Libraries. We owe special gratitude to Todd Belton, Peter Kaplan, and Virginia Shields for their support throughout the life of the project.

Special thanks to students who participated in the projects mentioned in this book:

Boston Chinatown: Angel Caballero, Tuan Phan, Margaret Wong, Fei Xing
SweatStats: Shana Diez, Stephen Carr, Marc Moesse, Adam Reynolds, Dan Itsara
Blitz: Catherine Chen, Edmund Chou, Tien-Lok Lau

Introduction

Bookstore shelves are packed with how-to manuals for designing and building Web pages and sites. These manuals may be written for the first-time author of a personal home page or for professional designers of corporate sites. No guide currently exists for the growing audience of instructors who must teach and practice the principles of communicating in cyberspace, in particular the principles of designing and building Web sites.

University courses on interactive communication and design are increasing in number along with the rapidly expanding curriculum of digital media studies. Yet currently available Web design manuals do not address this educational audience and their needs, focusing instead on specific, often technical instructions on how to engineer a particular look and feel as quickly as possible, given current technological dependencies. These books deal mainly with the appearance of the finished product and pay little attention to the ideas and processes involved in intelligent interactive design—processes that will remain unchanged long after certain technical competencies have vanished.

This guide addresses the needs of a growing audience of instructors and their students. It presents principles and examples of Web design with emphasis upon the process—rhetorical and technical—of design and implementation.

Organization

This book is organized in a roughly sequential manner following upon the authors' experiences teaching Web design. The book has been written to function both as a companion to a class, to be read incrementally over the span of several weeks, and as a handbook for independent study, to be read over a few days. Some parts are more "reference-like," while others are focused on specific planning and design processes such as content planning and information architecture.

Design Philosophy

In general, we feel that Web communications and design are not inherently different from other, less wired forms. Some authors feel that the "end of the printed page" is nigh and write elegies to books and reading. Other, more wired authors write panegyrics to digital media and the Web as if digital media were a new, miraculous life form. But in fact rhetorical principles that have defined communication over time apply equally well to the Web: a process of defining purpose, audience, and style to suit your objectives. We believe that this rhetorical process is also at the heart of most scientific and engineering projects: a careful mapping out of objectives, audience and technical approaches leading to design, implementation, testing and analysis—an iterative process.

We also believe that effective Web site design is an inherently collaborative process. Yes, personal home pages and some sites designed by individuals are outstanding. But our experiences suggest that building sites is a social, iterative process that requires not only technical skill but also more traditional communication skills, written and oral. This guide stresses a social, process-oriented approach to design and to successful classroom instruction.

1

Class Design and Curriculum

Since 1996—not long after Tim Berners-Lee created the World Wide Web—we have been teaching a popular undergraduate class in MIT's Writing Program called "Communicating in Cyberspace." In this class students (primarily undergraduates, but with several graduate students and visiting faculty as well) work in collaborative groups of four or five to propose, design, and implement Web sites. Our students quickly learn that successful communication in cyberspace is the result of a careful analysis of your objectives and audience; a collaborative effort among writers, designers, programmers, content developers, and managers; and a complicated dialogue with sponsoring clients. They learn that the mythology of hypertext ("interactive," user-authored texts that continually defy linear narrative) may be a fruitful source of theoretical discussion and a significant element in some uses of the Web. But they also see—once they are confronted with the demands of constructing a full-scale site—that elements of traditional rhetoric also apply.

Our students also learn that shadowing the technical process of creating a Web site is an equally important off-line process of hardcopy reports and formal and informal oral presentations. They learn that they must be able to communicate not only among themselves in their project groups, but also with their clients who may not share any of their technical competencies.

Why We Created This Class

The MIT course catalogue is filled with classes that study various pieces of Web communication: programming, graphic design, management, literary theory, rhetoric, comparative media studies. The value to such a curriculum is that each subject allows a student to focus closely on one particular piece of the puzzle, to develop a skill or analyze in depth theories of communication. But creating successful Web sites is a team effort, a collaborative process that integrates all the various skills of a production team. Individuals may assume different roles, but everyone must be able to collaborate with colleagues—and clients—throughout the whole production cycle.

We created this class to give our students a place to experiment with all aspects of Web site construction as part of a collaborative, team effort that mirrored the real world of Web design. Students learn to share their expertise throughout a semester-long group project that they propose, design, and implement. The class integrates seminar-style discussion, with presentations on a range of topics, and design workshops.

This approach was especially well suited to MIT—and we believe to other engineering and liberal arts schools—because MIT students like to apply their theoretical and abstract knowledge to real-world problems. Our students prefer to get their hands dirty in a lab rather than sitting passively in large lecture halls. We think most students want to apply their knowledge and to express their creativity by making something new. And the Web is an ideal medium for synthesizing technical knowledge and creativity.

Why a Writing Class?

Every large-scale engineering project takes shape through writing. Letters, memos, proposals, progress reports, and final reports document and to a large degree actually help invent many engineering and scientific projects. Scientists and engineers also make oral presentations (formal and informal) throughout the life of a project, and they must collaborate with other members of their research or design teams. Writing is the lifeblood of engineering and science.

The Web is quickly becoming one of our major communications media. But the Web is a dynamic medium of expression, changing, mutating rapidly as the underlying computing environment evolves. Any development of the World Wide Web is as dependent on writing and documentation as any other scientific or engineering project. As a new form of expression and communication, Web sites obviously include text and a variety of organizational styles. Web sites may represent texts in new ways, but writing—the complex matrix of activities alluded to when we use that word (audience analysis and focus, rhetorical form and organization, content, expressiveness, clarity)—is the heart of Web site construction.

The MIT Writing Program was, therefore, an excellent home for this course. The Program offers traditional writing classes in expository, non-fiction prose, creative writing, and technical and scientific writing. We understand how writing supports the design process in engineering and science, and we feel comfortable with creative and expressive forms of writing whether as poetry or essay, novel or drama, movie screenplay or radio show. We see every piece of writing as an experiment, a synthesis of theory and practice. Like all writing programs, we were a virtual "web" of texts and authors and collaborative enterprise before there was a Web.

Class Design and Curriculum

Large Web sites are designed and implemented by teams of people working in a collaborative environment. These individuals assume various well defined roles in the production cycle. This production cycle follows a designated timeline defined by milestones and reflected in a stream of written and oral presentations. Web design companies value the ability to communicate and collaborate with colleagues as much as technical competency.

We wanted to create a class that fostered this collaborative, team-based structure, a class that from beginning to end depended upon an individual's ability to work with others.

To achieve this objective, we structured our syllabus so that the entire production cycle required extensive practice in written and oral communication and peer review. We wanted a class that stressed face-to-face discussion of all aspects of project completion.

Use a Seminar-Style Class to Support Collaborative Work

We have used a small, seminar-style class to encourage dynamic, face-to-face peer review and discussion. We have limited class size to roughly sixteen students to achieve this objective. Class size over twenty tips the balance toward a presentational, lecture style of teaching. A class size below twenty fosters dialogue and interaction in real time, allowing every individual to participate in class discussion and project reviews. In addition, a small class size limits the number of group projects and ensures ample time to manage complete reviews of each project in class. A seminar approach also permits you to bring in guest lecturers to speak on various critical topics and fosters in-depth discussion of these subjects.

Find a Physical Space that Supports Collaborative Online Work

Cyberspace is usually discussed as a virtual, nonphysical environment, and the World Wide Web certainly does permit users to escape certain space and time restrictions in publishing and reviewing materials.

Web training and development, however, require specific real estate to support interaction. This requirement is nowhere more apparent than in educational contexts. Physical dimensions of your classroom will dictate certain limitations in your teaching style. We have learned that certain classroom configurations will not support the kind of teaching and interaction we recommend—indeed, some classroom designs definitely work against collaborative exchange.

Our classroom is outfitted with seventeen networked computers with Internet access. These computers ring the perimeter of the classroom, surrounding a central seminar table. Each workstation has a chair on rollers to permit students to turn easily from their on-screen work to face-to-face discussion around the table. The computer monitor is a very powerful focusing agent and it is important to be able to turn your back to it sometimes in order to engage in discussion.

The class is also equipped with an overhead, large-screen projection device to display the contents of the instructor's workstation on a screen at one end of the room. The instructor's computer is integrated into the ring of student workstations so that the instructor (or guest speaker) is assimilated into the discussion. Physical placement of this computer does not privilege the instructor in the flow of discussion. Students have repeatedly stated in end-of-semester evaluations that this classroom design encouraged them to assume more responsibility for discussion.

Design Your Class Around an Instructional Web Site

In addition to occupying a physical space, your class exists in cyberspace as well. A class Web site is a powerful although subtle instructional tool. We can identify several functions your class Web site should perform, including

• a public presentation of your subject, both within your school and to the world
• administrative support of certain key educational processes, including lists of assignments and topics, turning in of assignments, peer review, discussion, and reference

In some sense, a class supported by a Web site is always in session. In final class evaluations, students frequently comment that Web interactions (and other network-supported exchanges such as e-mail and class discussion lists) allowed them to continue and deepen intellectual discussions started in class around the seminar table. These asynchronous exchanges permit students to think a bit more carefully about their feelings and ideas regarding particular topics or project reviews.

Creating a class Web site is an excellent project for a project group to pursue.

Creating Your Syllabus

Figure 1.1 shows the opening page of the MIT class Web site, <http://web.mit.edu/21w785/www>.

Design Your Class Around Group Projects
The first two weeks of the semester focus on introductions: of possible projects and of individual students in the class. Students introduce themselves

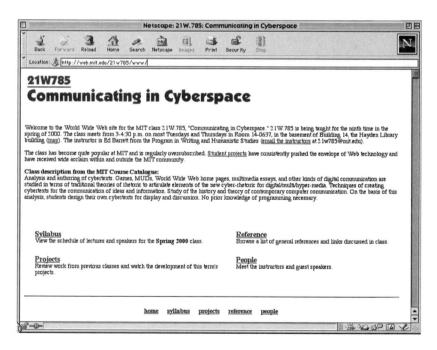

Figure 1.1
Opening page of our class web site.

as part of a roundtable discussion of possible projects. These introductions are primarily oral although you can encourage students to display their home pages on the large screen as well. In fact, you may require students to create a home page for this purpose. Some of these personal home pages will be quite advanced; others may be beginner's level. If this assignment is not given a letter grade, you can use this opportunity to encourage students to comment on each other's work in a helpful, constructive manner. In general, students who come to the class with rudimentary HTML skills have said that they learned valuable strategies and techniques for home page construction by looking at their peers' work.

Since class size is kept low, we interview each student out of class. These interviews are typically fifteen minutes long and touch on a variety of topics, with special emphasis on what they want to take away from this class, what skills they have, and project choices. The interview process is time-consuming, but it helps personalize the subject matter and may help the instructor figure out membership on a team. The personal interview, we have found, sets the tone for the rest of the semester.

As shown in figure 1.2, the first two weeks of the semester are devoted to the sometimes difficult process of establishing group projects. Two chief difficulties are encountered at this stage: (1) establishing teams, and (2) deciding on a team project.

In reality, these two processes are concurrent: students learn more about each other as they focus on a project. Each semester several projects have been sponsored by groups within MIT as well as by outside professional or corporate sponsors. There are definite benefits and drawbacks to projects sponsored in this way. In general, each semester student-inspired projects outweigh outside sponsored projects 3 to 1.

Structure Your Syllabus So that Students Learn an Iterative Approach to Design and Construction

Students must learn to structure their development projects around an iterative approach that allows their project to achieve greater focus and clarity as well as depth of content. Three obvious milestones help define this approach: the proposal, the progress report, and the final presentation. Each of these punctuation points in the life of a project can be further broken down into stages of development, each with a variety of report types to support it.

Week 1 — Introduction and Group Formation

Class 1
  Course overview
  Description of projects and roles
  Student introductions
Class 2
  Overview of site design process (includes charting the user experience and interviewing clients)
  Project group formation
  Reading for next class: look at past projects, begin preparing personal home page, familiarize yourself with HTML and Web technology (see `http://web.mit.edu/21w785/www/reference.html`)
  Assignment: submit a one-page description of term project; include a general description and a list of group members and roles

Week 2 — Group Formation, Audience, Focus, Metaphor

Class 1
  Discussion of past projects with students from previous classes
Class 2
  Web site planning: purpose, audience, and metaphor
  Assignment: review of home pages next week

Figure 1.2
Syllabus showing the first two weeks of the class devoted to building teams.

The Proposal

Alpha Design

As figure 1.3 shows, the first third of the semester is devoted to various stages of project proposal.

Initial student introductions, descriptions of possible projects, and out-of-class interviews are all elements of the initial proposal process. During this time, students freely brainstorm ideas among themselves, with time in class devoted to this. As always, we have found simple, face-to-face meetings among students to be the single most important element of this initial stage of the process. At the end of the second week of the semester, project groups should be formed and a brief, one-page statement of project, authored by the group, submitted for review by the instructor and for in-class discussion.

As part of group management, teams have defined roles for their individual members. In addition, each team should be required to establish an

Week 3 — Personal Home Page Review, Project Preplan

Class 1
Home page review
Elements of an oral presentation — informal "elevator speech," formal slide presentation
Reading for next class: read sections of
`http://web.mit.edu/is/discovery/discoverv.html#preplanning`
about project preplanning
Useful reference materials for next class: sample past project slide presentation for proposal

Class 2
Home page review
Creating project preplan site maps
Assignment: prepare site map poster

Week 4 — Project Preplan Poster Party

Class 1
Project preplan poster party
Assignment: prepare group oral alpha presentation

Week 5 — Alpha Presentations

Class 1
Alpha oral presentations
Class 2
Alpha oral presentations

Figure 1.3
The project proposal stage.

e-mail address for the project group to facilitate out-of-class communication with group members. By week 6 the proposal stage culminates with formal group oral and written presentations of project proposals.

Figure 1.4 shows a recommended structure for the oral and written proposals.

The Oral Presentation

Students should be required to create a Web slide show with visuals to communicate their project proposal simply and directly. Figure 1.5 is an example of a Web slide show used in a student project oral proposal.

The oral proposal provides all students with an opportunity to comment upon, and learn from, their peers. We have typically found that student comments on oral presentations during the Q&A period have provided project groups with valuable new ideas or technical suggestions.

Proposal Format

Front Matter

- Title page: name of project, names of team members, group email address, type of report (proposal), date
- Abstract: one paragraph, ca. 150 words; state problem, methods, expected results; no figures or references in abstract; do not use first person pronouns.
- Table of contents
- List of figures, if you have four or more

Body

- Introduction: background motivation for the project. This section establishes the need for the project; state primary and secondary audience.
- Statement of objectives: the clear objectives set for your project, purpose of the site; its scope
- Description of your project: make us "see" the project by describing proposed look and feel, design strategies you will employ, technical requirements, tools needed and how you will acquire them, platform/browser dependencies; plug-ins. Show a preliminary page mock-up.
- Tasks and milestones: show a graph which divides the life of the project into definable tasks (vertical axis) over time in weeks (horizontal axis). Punctuate the horizontal axis with important milestones you are expected to meet.
- Roles each team member will perform

End Matter
- References
- Appendices

Figure 1.4
Recommended structure for the oral and written proposals.

In addition to these public comments, we ask our students individually (and if they wish anonymously) to "grade" each group using a simple feedback form. These forms are not reviewed by the instructor but given directly to the group presenting. Students are encouraged to see themselves as active and responsible participants in the review process.

The Written Proposal
In addition to the oral proposal, students are asked to submit a ten-page written proposal. We have required group-authored proposals as a way of getting students to face critical issues of collaboration and group management. Although a student may be fulfilling the role of editor and content

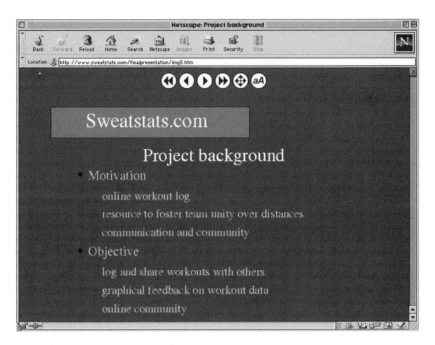

Figure 1.5
Sample web slide show used in student oral presentations.

gatherer, all students in a group are required to author sections of the proposal related to their chief area of responsibility.

Related Topics During the Proposal Stage
Supporting this initial design stage, ask students to review a variety of Web sites that encourage discussion and analysis of design strategies and techniques. These reviews will help students in another important initial design step, creating a site map. Site maps, authored by the group, are especially useful as a brainstorming and focusing tool. We ask students to present these in an informal poster session preceding the final proposal as another, preliminary review tool. Figure 1.6 shows an example of an informal site map.

The Progress Report, Beta Design
The next milestone in the design process is an oral progress report showing a beta stage of each team's site design. Figure 1.7 shows the specifications we require for this report.

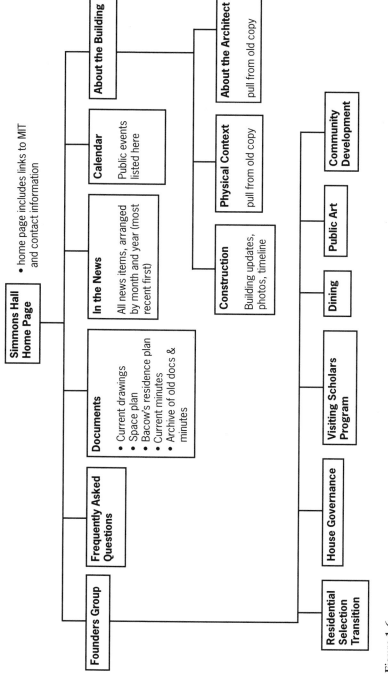

Figure 1.6
Example of preliminary site map.

Progress Report Format

A progress report is a managerial tool—it allows someone to assess how things are going. A progress report is also a very useful crisis point for your project as you recognize and deal with the important problems every design project encounters. Clients expect that you will encounter problems and that certain rosy predictions of the long-ago proposal will have been modified (within reason) to suit reality. The subtext of every progress report is to instill confidence in a client that you will get the job done.

Elements of this oral report

Time limits: 15 minutes (max.) for presentation; five minutes for Q&A.

1. Introduction
- State title of project and names of presenters.
- Reiterate motivation, scope, and statement of objectives (tell us if your original objectives or scope of project has changed since the proposal, and why). Brief restatement of motivation; objectives are more important.

2. Body
- Present current state of activities: TWO key questions:
  1) What have you accomplished so far?
  2) What remains to be done?
- State any changes in technical requirements for project development or for intended audience to view it.
- Identify key problems encountered and how solved—if not resolved what effects will that have? Management/group dynamics? Changes in your proposed look and feel.
- DEMO! DEMO! DEMO! Show us current state of design.
  Explain all changes from proposal.

3. End
- Show the progress you have achieved by reference to a revised time chart.
- Indicate what looming catastrophes you expect and how you expect to resolve these crises.
- Make us feel confident that you have been working on the project and accomplishing your objectives in the time proposed, and that it will be completed on time.

4. Q & A

Figure 1.7
Recommended structure for the progress report.

Typically, this report takes place about four weeks after the proposal. Students during this time have incorporated instructor's comments and peer reviews into their design. In addition, students continue to discuss certain key topics as presented by guest speakers.

The Final Presentation
Time at the end of the semester is reserved for crucial in-class group meetings and technical roundtable discussions to help with final project implementation. These group meetings are very important to the success of the final project. In general, students underestimate the time needed to achieve certain project milestones. Even the best-managed team project runs into trouble at this point in the semester; close supervision by the instructor through informal group meetings can help a project succeed.

Figure 1.8 shows the specifications for the final written and oral presentations. Elements of the final oral presentation can be adapted from the progress report.

Finally, figure 1.9 shows the relative weight we give to these assignments.

Class Web Site

A class Web site is a key part of any Web design class, and, increasingly, many other classes as well. Since the day we began teaching our class, we have used a homegrown Web site to fulfill a variety of duties, from providing a syllabus and handouts to collecting assignments. In this chapter, geared to instructors and class site designers, we discuss important features of a class Web site and how to implement them.

An increasing number of college classes use Web sites as instructional aides. Class Web sites in general serve two important purposes—to extend the accessibility of traditional class materials and to facilitate student-student and student-instructor interaction. A site for a class about Web design has additional specific purposes to serve because the site offers students a unique opportunity to learn about a medium through that same medium.

Final Project Report Format

Length: 10–12 pages minimum

Front Matter

- Title Page: Name of project, URL, type of report, contributors, location, date
- Abstract: One paragraph (ca. 150 words), problem, methods, results/conclusions/recommendations (the whole report in miniature; no figures or references in abstract)
- Table of Contents (all headings in report appear here)
- List of Figures (if more than four)

Body

- Introduction: Background/motivation and intended audience(s) for your project. Leads to statement of objective and general description of your overall design
- Technical Approach: Design choices; tools used; platform dependencies (if any); what you needed to implement the design. Accommodations for different browsers. Performance issues
- Description of Design (with figures in written report; demo in oral report): Overall metaphor for the design. Look and feel. How it works, user scenario(s). Navigation. Links to other sites and why
- Evaluation of design in light of motivation: Problems; what you had to leave undone (if anything)–what you did that didn't work and effects on project; studies of users. Project management: were your time estimates realistic?
- Conclusions/Recommendation for future work: What needs to be done by next project group; how best to maintain site

End Matter

- Acknowledgments (if any)
- References: hardcopy and Web references
- Appendices (documentation of programming when appropriate)

Figure 1.8
Recommended structure for the final presentation.

Assignment	Weight
class participation	25%
includes attendance, questions and responses for speakers, and participation in discussions	
proposals and presentations	35%
includes one-page proposal, storyboard poster, oral presentations and notes, and written proposal	
final presentation and assessment of project	40%
includes final project presentation, final written report, and final project exhibition	

Figure 1.9
Relative weight given to all presentations throughout the semester.

Basic Features of a Class Web Site

As with any project that seeks to reproduce existing information on the Web, a class site must provide up-to-date copies of all relevant standard class information. This information will often include the following:

- contact information (e-mail, Web)
- class times and locations (and maps)
- syllabus
- assignments
- references
- roster (usually restricted to class participants)

In many cases, these documents already exist in digital form, and it is short work to collect them together for a small Web site using basic conversion tools or word processors. Of course, these pages can be further enhanced by adding links to other Web resources.

The class Web site provides an easy way to store and disseminate basic class information, but don't expect the information to update itself. Building a class Web site is hardly a one-time affair, and effort must be devoted to keeping the content up-to-date. It is useful to spend a little more time in the beginning thinking about organization and formatting so as to save time later on when the site must be refreshed.

Here are a few more tips for the basic class Web site:

• It is better to convert a document electronically to HTML than provide a scanned-in version of it.
• If there is proprietary or class-only information on the site, be sure to protect it.
• Make sure that the site is reliable—if it's on your own server, take measures to ensure its reliability and check up on it regularly.
• Always keep printed versions of any essential documents on the Web site.
• Make sure your pages are easy to print out (avoid light backgrounds; use readable type sizes and graphics).

But why the Web? What is the advantage of putting the information on the Web if students are going to receive it in class anyway? Ignoring the advantages of instant accessibility, one advantage of a Web site is the potential for increased communication.

The easiest way to achieve that goal is to pepper the site with opportunities for feedback to the instructors or other staff, possibly using a mailto link on the class home page. Questions about the syllabus? Send e-mail to the professor. Not sure about an assignment? E-mail the TA.

A couple of e-mail lists might also come in handy, one for the instructors and one consisting of all the students and the instructors.

Assignment Turn-In

A more advanced feature for a class Web site is the ability for students to turn in assignments over the Web. This could be as simple as e-mailing or posting a URL, or something more complicated involving an ongoing portfolio of student submissions.

In our class, we have used an assignment turn-in facility to track students' work. From the syllabus or a listing of assignments, the student would follow a link to a simple form with an assignment "prompt" and a space for adding or editing a response. Information about the assignment—including date due, background information, and relevant URLs—was provided at the top of the form.

2

Team-Based Web Design

Professional Web sites are not designed by only one person—unless the site is meant to be used by only one user! A good Web site is always the work of many people. Sites designed by individuals often suffer from tunnel vision—the site seems to be organized and operates just fine from the designer's point of view, but other people find it confusing and difficult to use.

Members of a project will adopt various roles and responsibilities to create the site. The descriptions below are designed to give an overview of possible roles team members could fulfill—the actual organization will vary from project to project, and in almost every case, people will take on two or three roles each. Several people might even share a role.

Team Size

In general, we have found that a team composed of four or five students is ideal. If a team has under four members, it is insufficiently staffed. If the team has over five people, it becomes unwieldy and risks not functioning well.

Why Identify Roles?

Clarifying roles, and understanding how to interact within a team, is very important to the success of the class project and to success in the real world. Employers want students who are technically competent and can work well with others. Roles evolve within a team; someone who is good at a particular role will share his or her expertise with the rest of the team, and the team learns as it works. Roles can also be shared. A fine line exists between collaboration and stepping on someone's toes. Problems are minimized with clear communications and an understanding of process.

Individuals in teams sometimes see problems—and their solutions—through the lens of their own particular area of expertise. It is essential that you gather different viewpoints and come to a clear understanding of the reasoning behind your choices. A Web site has to function for many people, not just one person. Each discipline's solution to a problem may not be the best for the end user. The creative friction between the visions of different professions—programmer, graphic designer, writer—can make your site a richer experience for the intended audience.

Each team in the class discusses the expertise of the individuals in the group and explores an initial mapping between that expertise and the roles listed below. Notice that the role of Webmaster is missing from the list. This word has become a catch-all for any of the activities described above, and thus has lost unique meaning. Another problematic word is *designer*. Does this mean graphic design? System architecture and design? Interaction design? The words *webmaster* and *designer* are useful only when combined with a second defining role, such as Webmaster/System Administrator.

One risk in assigning roles is that even with a team, one individual may end up burdened with too many responsibilities, sometimes even by choice. It's up to the manager to ensure that everybody has a manageable workload and the responsibilities are equitably and practically distributed. The interdependencies of many different parts of the site production process mean that one slipped deadline may have repercussions across the entire group. Assigning multiple people to cover some roles may also help avoid this risk.

Strategies to Facilitate Teamwork

1. Clearly define the goals and process.
2. Encourage individuals with particularly exceptional competencies to take on roles in areas they have not mastered—while coaching others in their areas of expertise.
3. Identify roles to help move a discussion forward when there are conflicting ideas of how to proceed. This removes the discussion from the personal point of view to the perspective of a discipline.
4. Define project phases, milestones, and deadlines to help the team to focus.
5. Co-author project documents to encourage discussion of problem areas. We allow class time for the teams to discuss their projects; this may be the only opportunity the students have for face-to-face interaction.
6. Set up interactive tools such as group mailing lists and instant messaging communications.

Table 2.1
Team Roles in Web Site Development

Role	Skills/Responsibilities
Project Manager	The project manager facilitates communications and is responsible for focusing the team's attention of their goals and schedule.
Client Representative	Understands the problem statement, the business environment in which this Web site will operate; knows the best practices in the industry, and competition. This person interviews clients and writes business requirements for the site (i.e., the context or service desired).
Technology Researcher	Investigates the appropriate technology for the site, such as search engines, Internet service providers, databases.
Content Developer	Writer, editor. Skilled at achieving the right tone and voice for the Web site. For those sites relying on content not already prepared for the Web (most sites have at least some of this content), the content developer will gather and process this content. Content developers will be involved with scanning text pages and collecting and converting video and still images; they will often work closely with a liaison for a particular content source to determine the nature of the content and tools and time required for preparation. Content developers should be familiar with the tools and technologies (cameras, scanners, image conversion software) required to prepare the content for the Web. They may work with the multimedia and technical designers to establish conversion procedures and data formats for the site.
Writer	All sites have some kind of original content, even if it's just the home page and help text. Writers create this text, following basic style guidelines and conventions. A writer will present the content with a certain "voice" as desired by the site design plan.
Information Architect	The information architect is involved in the first phase of site design—organizing the content and mapping out the relationships between content areas and individual pages. The information architect will work with visual and technical designers to build the site's navigation system and other basic interactive features. The information architect's goal is to produce a clear, coherent site design—well-organized, easily navigable, and with understandable content.

Table 2.1 (continued)

Role	Skills/Responsibilities
Graphic Designer	Graphic designer, illustrator. Responsible for the visual identity of the site, the layout of the pages, navigation elements, and so forth. Graphic designers create the appearance, the interface look and feel for the site's pages and interactive features. Graphic designers will use graphic creation and manipulation software as well as Web page editors to produce design templates for each page and page component, as well as the interfaces to the interactive features. Graphic designers will need to coordinate their work with the multimedia and technical designers to ensure a consistent look and feel for the entire site.
Multimedia Designer	Some sites may require multimedia content beyond basic still images. If your site includes prepared video or audio content (streaming, pushed, or downloaded), you will need a multimedia designer to work with the content gatherer to develop the proper formatting and delivery technology for such content. The multimedia designers will also create features for the site as required. Multimedia designers should be familiar with a range of multimedia design tools, both for traditional video and audio as well as more sophisticated Web animation and interactive client technologies.
Technical Designer	In the design phase of the project, the technical designer's job is to choose technologies to implement the site's interactive features, and to develop working prototypes of those features. The technical designer will often also be the person who builds the applications (the programmer). The technical designer will be familiar with typical programming languages including JavaScript, Java, Perl, and C; an understanding of user interaction principles and interface design is also useful.
Production	Responsible for converting the original data and images into HTML (or equivalent) pages. The actual application of the visual design templates to the content is the process by which most of the pages on the site will be produced. The content producers will be responsible for assembling the pages for the site. They will work closely with the programmers to properly integrate the technical features into the pages, and to apply the visual design templates to the interactive application interfaces. This role will almost certainly be shared among several people, all of whom will have other roles as well.

Table 2.1 (continued)

Role	Skills/Responsibilities
Programmer/System Administrator	Web site engineer. The programmer is responsible for fully developing, testing, and deploying the interactive features prototyped by the technical designer (who will often be the same person). Programmers will need to work with server administrators to ensure smooth behind-the-scenes operation of their applications. Programmers will require the same skills as technical designers; additionally, depending on the site's size, an understanding of Web servers and advanced application programming systems (database integration and application servers) will be useful. The system administrator runs the server and backend programs, schedules backups, and handles security issues.
Tester/Focus Group Coordinator	Quality assurance: tests the usability of the site from the user's point of view and the robustness of the code. Your site will need someone to coordinate the focus group used for audience research, design reviews, and final testing. This person could be the manager, but doesn't have to be. He or she should be familiar with the site's plan and its evolving design, as well as general Web issues and typical user concerns. The focus group coordinator will be responsible for communicating the focus group comments and suggestions to the rest of the design team. Again, the role doesn't have to be filled by only one person—a different person can coordinate different focus groups, and each group can have more than one coordinator.
Web Page Publisher/Editor	Ongoing care and feeding of the content of the site. The editor's task is to review all of the site's content to ensure a consistent style and approach. Beyond typos and grammar errors, the editor should also look for style mismatches (changes of voice and person), visual design conflicts, and other inconsistencies. Generally, several people will edit and review a site to make sure all the problems are caught.

Successful teamwork is based on the difference between "team work" and a site "designed by a committee." Remember, the site should be usable by the intended audience, not just by the design team.

Building a Web site presents an excellent learning opportunity, so there will always be some overlap between the various roles whether by accident or design. Site planning, design, and construction should always happen as a unified team effort, so that each person will have a general idea of where the other members of the team stand with their work. Very few parts of the design process are totally independent; team interaction will help alleviate tie-ups and dependencies and allow individuals to juggle the priorities to keep the site production on track.

3

Planning a Web Site

This chapter will present the planning process map to help you achieve your desired objectives. The planning phase of creating a Web site is the process of clearly mapping out the site's "big picture" and identifying resources before committing to a specific content organization and visual design. In many cases, predesign planning happens in a scattered and ad hoc fashion, with predictable results: missed project deadlines, midstream corrective redesigns, inconsistent site structure, tacked-on features, and just plain poorly built sites.

Process Map

Professional Web design studios follow a defined process in planning a site.

Set Your Objectives for the Site

Defining objectives is not as easy as it sounds. You may have a general idea for what you want to do and what the site will accomplish, which sounds perfectly coherent and exciting to the team in the discussion stage. As you approach design, however, you now have to take your ideas and creative energies and think about engineering ways to express and achieve them.

For example, the goals for the official MIT site (<http://web.mit.edu>) are to

- promote the MIT identity
- provide users with a greater ability to find MIT information
- facilitate work processes at MIT with Web-based applications
- make better use of content to showcase MIT's strengths

What need is the Web site going to solve?   For example, a class Web site fulfills a student's needs to find out what activities are going to take place and when certain assignments are due and what reference materials are available. A faculty member needs to have a clear statement of the course requirements and how those requirements will be met. Untitled, a poetry Web archive, initially conceived of the need for an extensive repository of poetry by a wide range of authors from many time periods. In fact, the team discovered through the development process that this need for reference material was probably secondary to the need for visitors to exchange and discuss original poems, perhaps within the larger historical context that the site originally intended to present.

What questions would users bring to the site, in the hope of finding an answer?   At this stage, members of the project team can act as surrogates for their users and make a list of these questions. Professional designers generally like to use active verbs in stating the answers to these questions. For example, "the student *will find* the hours the pool is open," or "the user *will purchase and download*" an article. These questions will be used to test the navigation and functions below.

Define Your Site's Identity
For all of its complexity and extension through the Internet, Web sites that have a readily identifiable character or identity have a chance at success. In order to define your project site's identity, discuss these questions with your team members.

What is the key message the site will convey?   By key message we mean a succinct phrase that is the "aha" experience you want the audience to get. Key messages should not be long-winded explanations. They are succinct and repeatable. You'll know your site is successful if users of the site can easily state this message, even in their own words. For example, slashdot.org presents "News for nerds. Stuff that matters."

A key message is not a slogan, so don't worry about rhymes or making it a catchy phrase. If you had to communicate a thought in a headline, what would you say? Some faculty at the MIT Sloan School of Management use the phrase "elevator speech" to refer to the succinctness and punch necessary for getting across your ideas in a narrowly defined time period. If you wanted to pitch an idea to someone while in an elevator between the third and fifth floors, what would you say?

What is the metaphor for the site?   Define the feeling of your site using abstract language, to define qualities as opposed to features. List some adjectives describing the design. How do you want the audience/users to feel?

Two examples on the MIT site clarify the concept of using a metaphor on your Web site. First, consider the Web site for the Department of Mechanical Engineering at <http://me.mit.edu> as shown in figure 3.1.

The site uses puzzle pieces as a metaphor for the department. The metaphor is solving puzzles and putting the picture together. The puzzle pieces work not because they are a literal representation of the department, but because they are an abstract—and humorous—representation of an engineering skill.

The second example is the Department of Foreign Languages and Literature Web site, also at MIT, <http://web.mit.edu/fll/www> as shown in figure 3.2.

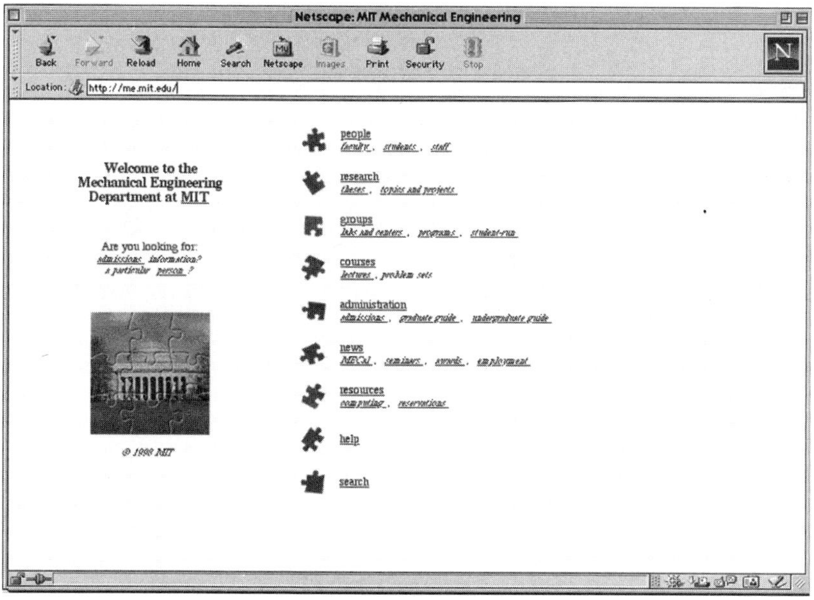

Figure 3.1
Web site for the MIT Department of Mechanical Engineering.

Figure 3.2
Web site for the MIT Department of Foreign Languages and Literature.

The site designers discussed the essential motivation of the target audience, and "why someone would want to learn a foreign language." The answer they chose is "to communicate." The top page displays beautifully rendered stamps that represent the languages taught by the department. The metaphor is continued throughout the site, giving structure that is not meant to be overtly perceived by the user, but nevertheless ties together the experience on the site. For instance, faculty biographies are displayed as letters received (figure 3.3); projects are in the form of postcards (figure 3.4). Additionally, each language page presents content in English and in the respective foreign language.

Describe Primary and Secondary Audiences
Although anyone on the Internet can look at a public site, you'll want to reach people who will appreciate your Web site, its services, and its content. In economic terms, you want to reach customers who will buy your product. You're not excluding anyone, but you are attempting, at this stage, to identify your primary and secondary audiences.

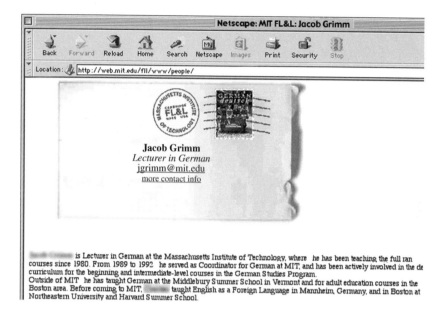

Figure 3.3
Use of metaphor: Faculty biographies in the MIT Department of Foreign Languages and Literature displayed as letters.

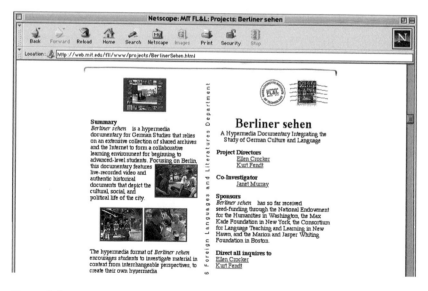

Figure 3.4
Use of metaphor: Research projects in the MIT Department of Foreign Languages and Literature displayed as postcards.

Figure 3.5
Home page for SweatStats.

SweatStats (figure 3.5) is a site for logging one's personal workout times in various sports, on an individual, team, or league basis. While anybody might visit the site from a particular school to see how his or her team is doing, the site's primary audience is athletes involved in competition and training. Identifying this particular audience and its preferences will help in designing the site and making decisions in the process.

Project teams should be able to describe not just the technical capabilities their audiences may possess; they also need to describe the demographics of their intended audiences, who they are and what they may know. Age, gender, education, profession, and level of familiarity with online communication are key elements to identify. Primary audiences are users who have a strong need for visiting a particular site. Secondary audiences of course could be almost any casual Web surfer, but in general we define a secondary audience as one who checks in on a site from time to time without a pressing need to fulfill.

When identifying future student prospects, MIT researched the publications high schoolers were reading, what they thought was cool. In other words, they wanted to identify their *expectations* based on cultural practices. Audience expectations are subjective and feature-oriented, driven by popular culture and related or competing Web sites.

Expectations, however, are of secondary importance to identifying your audience's needs. Needs are the fundamental reason, or reasons, why members of your audiences will visit the site. A need could be to get admissions guidelines for a school, to learn about the Boston Chinatown community, to take a virtual reality (VR) tour of a place, or to play an interactive game, for example. Considering the needs of your primary audience will help you define content and functions on your site. In this planning phase, reexamine the site's proposed purpose from a visitor's point of view: what questions and problems they would want the site to resolve?

It is important to realize that in this planning phase the stated purpose of your site will also act as a focusing agent for an audience's needs as well. If, for example, your project proposal states that your site will offer a complete reference guide to poetry, visitors will be unhappy to find anything less. Setting up such an expectation and then not fulfilling it will drive visitors from your site.

Correctly identifying core audience needs may also point to other features your site should provide. These related features often answer major additional audience expectations. For example, a student project for online registration must have a method for ensuring private and secure transactions as well as a fully searchable course catalog—expectations derived from experience with both offline registration procedures as well as any online retail site.

Use a Focus Group to Define Needs and Expectations

Focus groups are composed of users who will be representative of your intended audience. You can ask them specific questions about expectations and technical capabilities. A random, representative user group of six or seven people will suffice. Bring in this focus group at the start of the project, and later for design reviews and ultimately to test-drive the completed site. Colleagues and friends may not be the best people to ask to serve as a focus group, nor should you use your own project group because you may not be sufficiently critical in answering key questions since you may unconsciously feel as if you already have the answers. Ask the focus group questions about their needs, expectations, level of content familiarity, technical resources, and expertise. Encourage back-and-forth discussions, and be sure to note any suggestions.

You may start a focus group planning discussion by talking about what features users would expect to find on a site. But this tactic serves primarily as a means of establishing fundamental expectations and needs—the reasons they would visit, the processes they would want to transact, what the site would do for them. A focus group may also be helpful in establishing contradictory purposes for visiting the site. For example, a VR tour of MIT would not necessarily contain links to registration or admission pages.

Finally, a focus group is an excellent means for sketching out presumed familiarity with your site's content. This information can be used to determine preliminary navigational techniques and information architecture. You may present them with certain topics or categories and ask them if they belong in the site, and if so, where they might place them. Some of these categories may become navigational links later on.

Low-tech methods are quite useful in obtaining this information from focus groups in the planning phase. For example, when designers were planning a revamping of the MIT site, they sat around a small conference table with a small focus group and presented group members with a stack of yellow sticky-note pads. They asked the individuals to write down the kinds of information they expected to find on this site. After weeding out repetitive notes, they asked the group to begin categorizing or grouping the remaining notes into related stacks on a large whiteboard. These initial groupings were reviewed and then revised in subsequent discussion. The process was reiterated several times and quickly converged on a stable set of top-level categories for the home page.

In addition to broken links or the need for plug-ins in order to get essential information, site developers try to minimize cultural faux pas that might alienate a primary or secondary audience. For example, an early project in our class, the MIT Online Women's Site, wanted to use a ribbon image as a footer for each page. This ribbon was color-coded to indicate the section of the site users were on. The designers inadvertently chose pink for the home page. Luckily they tested the site early on and realized their unconscious use of a culturally loaded symbol.

What Are Your Audience's Technical Resources and Level of Comfort?
In addition to determining an audience's needs and expectations, correctly estimating their technical resources and level of comfort is critical to plan-

ning a successful site. This will determine the degree of design complexity and advanced technology you can use on your site, including multimedia and special markup tags. You must be able to estimate your audience's resources, including browser platform, bandwidth, and expected familiarity with various plug-ins.

You will have to determine if your audience will be accessing your site with traditional mainstream browsers or nontraditional platforms (WebTV, handhelds). Focus groups can be asked about browser preference as well as the chief location at which they will be accessing your site (work, school, home). Each locale will probably present them with a different choice of platforms. You should ask them what version of browser software they use and how comfortable they feel about upgrading to a later version or installing additional software to access certain kinds of information.

Be careful not to assume that your audience will use the same platform you are designing on. You will need to test your site on other platforms as well. Many student presentations fall flat because the platform they work on is different from the platform used in the classroom as well as different from the instructor's choice of platform at home. Or sometimes a fine project is useless because it is created with bleeding-edge technology for an audience (e.g., a grade school classroom) that does not have access to the same technology.

In the planning phase, you are chiefly concerned with setting the baseline for all members of your primary audience. And it is usually safest to go with the lowest common denominator and build from there.

Estimate what the slowest expected network connection will be. The network transmission speed, or bandwidth (measured in the number of kilobytes of data sent in a second), available to your audience is a critical limiting factor in design. Network traffic is always determined by the weakest link—if your server has a high-speed Internet connection but your audience is using a slow modem, your pages will load only as fast as the slowest part of the connection can send them. Asking your focus group at this stage what kinds of connections its members have will give you an idea how fast they can access your site.

You should also determine the locations from which your focus group members will primarily access your site. If from a private residence you may expect a range of modem speeds. In general you can expect a current baseline of 28.8k or 33.6k on home modems although more recently computers have been shipped with built-in 56k modems, which slightly exceeds the

FCC's maximum allowed speed for telephone lines of 53.6k. Some users in major cities have had access to ISDN (integrated services digital network) at 64k and 128k, and more recently, DSL (digital subscriber line) and cable modem service (often referred to as "broadband" connections) running at speeds over 700k.

If your audience will be accessing your site from a corporate or university network, they will have a theoretical maximum bandwidth of several million bits per second. However, all access speeds are "theoretical" and affected by the number of users online at the same time. In some corporate environments or other "intranet" sites, users connect to the Internet via a firewall or proxy server, which may restrict the type of connection they can make, connection speed, and time of access.

Don't Confuse Your Client with Your Audience
Most projects in the real world have a sponsoring client. A sponsoring client is not necessarily your primary audience although you should question your clients about what audiences they seek to reach. For one class project, the client was *The Boston Globe* newspaper, but the intended audience was not the managing editors or publisher, but young readers with a college education interested in careers in health. The client is usually the person footing the bill, or a person who works for the person paying the bills. For this reason they are basically calling the shots although they may not be intimately involved with all aspects of design and implementation.

It is important to identify clients so you can keep them informed of the directions the project is taking and to manage their expectations as well as align the directions of the project to their goals. If possible, the student team should interview a client to get at the business processes, to find out what will constitute success for the client. Don't leave the client behind—the Web site is not successful unless the client is satisfied.

When interviewing the client, if you hear something you think won't work, don't react in a negative fashion. Ask the client "why" he or she is asking for that feature. Understanding someone's reasoning can help you get at the real goal and possibly solve her problem in a better way.

Identify and Prioritize Content and Functions
Content and functionality are critical elements in the success of a site. But content is rarely just a collection of facts or undigested data. Content is a

complex matrix of "information" and expressive ability. All of the sup-
posedly minor formatting and layout decisions you make affect a user's
understanding of a site's content.

The site's purpose, from the visitor's perspective, should be clearly conveyed on the top page. Write the content from the user's perspective, so they
can readily see "what's in it for me."

What is the content "hook" to engage the primary and secondary audiences? Like a key message discussed above, a "hook" grabs a visitor's attention and makes the reader want to read on. An example can be seen on
MIT's Capital Campaign site, <http://web.mit.edu/campaign> (figure 3.6),
that leads with the phrase "Knowing where to put the X." When you click
on that, a story unfolds of an MIT alum who used his expertise to diagnose
a problem and marked the problem spot with an "X."

Writing Style
The Web is—in the year 2001—still primarily a textual environment, writing the most critical element in Web communications. By writing we mean

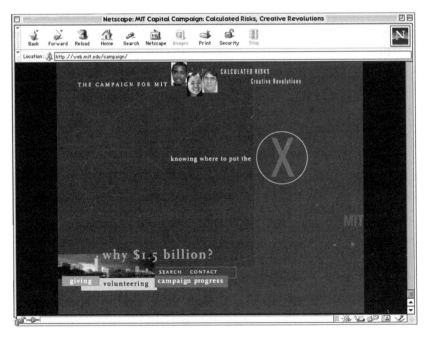

Figure 3.6
MIT's Capital Campaign page.

more than creating "content," as if content could ever be separated from the form in which it is created and conveyed. Writing style should never be confused with mere ornamentation, a sort of window dressing that is "added on" after your site has been created. Attention to matters of style in written (as well as visual) communication should begin at the inception of any Web project.

Your style of writing must suit your purpose.   As we have discussed, Web developers begin by identifying their chief objectives for their site. You may be offering a tour of a region or a portal to other sites or a place to enter and compare data for specific uses. The tone and style of your verbal content should not undermine your purpose. A site offering a campus tour to prospective applicants would not employ the same sort of language as would a page for current students wishing to get class registration information. A site offering medical information would not be effectively served by a style that might be used to sell this year's line of SUVs.

Your style of writing must suit your audience.   Early in your site development process, you defined your primary and secondary audiences in terms of demographics and technical expertise. You should also define the style of writing most appropriate to these prospective users. A medical site for doctors seeking information on specific pathologies would use a different level of diction and sentence structure than would a site aimed at the nonspecialist who wants to know what the symptoms of food poisoning are. Failure to match your style of writing to your audience will undermine confidence in your site.

Your style of writing must support effective hyperlinking.   Writing for the Web involves another element of style: how to and when to provide links to other pages within your site, or in some cases on other sites. Writing for the Web in this case is like writing in 3-D: not only do you move your reader from word to word down the screen, you also have to plan when best to give your reader the chance to move to another information space. This consideration is certainly related to elements of information architecture and navigation (see chapter 4). But you must also wrestle with creating passages that allow the visitor to your site to get all the content of a particular paragraph (for example) while also making that paragraph a jumping-off spot for related content. The writer must decide how much information is relevant to a particular passage, how much can be placed on another page, and how to help the reader forecast if a link is worth following right now.

Successful writers, therefore, master the art of describing (quickly and effectively) what a linked word or phrase connects to, and whether the link is within the current site or off it. A Web writer must be able to imagine how far from a particular link a user may go once he or she has opened the exit door. Yes, the mythology of hypertext stresses free exploration and user-authored texts. In reality, this mythology is often an excuse for poor planning. And since current Web browsers do not offer effective annotation tools beyond simplistic bookmarking, users rarely keep track of where they have been, either within a site or when surfing from one site to another—in other words, they do not "author" anything. Failure to provide textual clues about current and prospective destinations within a site will cause you to lose your audience.

Another element of style is also critical here. Some users prefer to have links shown within phrases and sentences as they read a passage; some users would prefer to have these links gathered into a coherent set presented, with appropriate descriptions, at the end of a page or section of a page. For example, in a one-page résumé on the Web you might identify the lab or firm where you worked one semester and give the link to that firm at the end of the employment section.

Your style of writing should respond to the current "culture" of similar Web sites. In the planning stage of site development, you should check out your presumed competition to determine what stylistic elements they employ. In this sense, this process is like identifying the particular genre of sites your team wishes to join. If your site is aimed at Web-savvy college students, you probably can employ a selection of key, abbreviated phrases and jargon where appropriate and expected although nothing ages faster than Web jargon, and sometimes an audience can respond positively to a new element of style that shakes them out of their expectations.

Your style of writing must be consistent in tone. Whatever elements of style you decide upon, you should employ them consistently throughout your site. Formal diction on one page turning unexpectedly into slang on another page will suggest to a user that the content on your site has not been thoroughly developed or reviewed.

Your style of writing can be made more complex as your audience goes deeper into the site. The MIT home page contains only a handful of words yet offers visitors entry into a site that contains approximately one million pages of content. As the user drills down into the site, the texture of expression deepens to suit the complexity of content. Users are rarely patient when entering a site. If your style of writing on a top-level page is dense (because of overly complex syntax or too rapid a pace of information transfer), chances are your visitor will not easily digest the material nor be inclined to go deeper into the site. Users expect that sublevel pages will contain more in-depth information, and they will be more inclined to spend time reading more complicated prose.

Your style of writing should be error-free. No one would ever mistake the breezy, almost militantly upbeat tone of most Web communications with the hallowed halls of whatever institution you want to insert here. Yet the general level of education of Web users is above average and some habits, luckily, are slow to die. We have been surprised at how quickly our students nail misspellings and obvious grammatical errors when they critique Web sites. A page might be on the big screen for ten seconds, yet half the class jumps on an error missed by the development team. Needless to say, if your site is meant to sound authoritative, nothing undermines your authority more quickly than substituting "it's" for "its." Such errors can be especially fatal in Web publication of résumés.

Look at the Competition

Identifying the features of related or competing sites not only serves to provide a list of features to implement—you will also find ways to distinguish your site from the others by providing features they lack, or by improving their features.

Sometimes the competitive site is not in your industry but is a site known to your defined audience that has set their expectations. For instance, a small museum online shop will be judged and compared to larger e-commerce sites that have already impacted some of the same users. Identify sites that could be considered competitive sites, evaluate them, and specify how your site will distinguish itself from them.

Discuss the Graphic Design

At the planning stage you'll want to begin to identify graphical directions for further exploration. What are several possible design directions for the site? For example, your site could have a brochure look and feel relying on photographs and textual design layout; alternately, it could have hand-drawn images and use the metaphor of an art gallery.

Identify existing images you might have to build upon. Are you building on existing graphical systems or creating a new one? Is there a logo or trademark to be used?

At this stage, try to keep your discussions at a relatively abstract level; describe the desired tone and effect of the design rather than selecting a specific item too quickly. This will lead to more possibilities being considered, and maybe a more effective design.

Navigation

When using a Web site, a user may choose the order of movement, but the paths she or he can possibly take are determined in advance by the designers of the site. If you provide too many options, the navigation is confusing. If you provide too few, it is perceived to be hard or inadequate. If a site locks you in or leads to blind alleys, the user will leave the site with the worst of impressions.

Create a site map to develop good navigation. For each of the defined audience groups, create a scenario of a person using the site to fulfill that person's goals. Test your site's navigation scheme by imagining how that audience will answer the questions. It's not enough to prove that the question is answered; the *way* in which it's answered is as important as the answer, since it defines the experience the user will have on your site.

Identify the group of functions that are important to have on every page; these should be part of a consistent menu or navigation system. Does your site need secondary menus?

Orientation is also important. What visual cues will let users know where they are on the site? Make sure each page is identified as being part of the larger site. Don't forget to ensure that if the user prints any page, the printout will identify the source and lead them to your Web site.

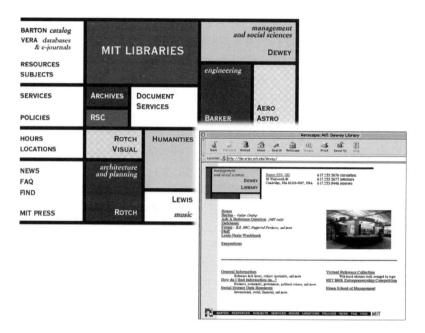

Figure 3.7
Use visual cues to let users know where they are on your site.

Team Roles

Chapter 2 described the various roles each team member can play on the project. Identify what your strengths are, and what new skills you'd like to learn in this process.

Design and Production Schedule

As with any project, a schedule is key to getting the work done and to avoiding conflict of unclear expectations. As part of the planning process, each student group agrees upon a schedule and posts it on its project page on the class Web site. Figure 3.8 shows a schedule posted by a project group; milestones and duration of tasks are clearly shown.

Testing and Evaluation

Testing is used throughout the Web design and development cycle. In early stages of the design, testing your design and user interface assumptions with users gives you real-world feedback and provides you with the opportunity to fine-tune your assumptions. In the middle stages of development, testing

Task	Resp	Assist	Duration	May 1, '00		May 22, '00		Jun 12, '00		Jul 3, '00	
				T	F	S	S	M	T	W	T	F	S	S
Designer Selected			0 w											
Discuss Look and Feel			1.4 w											
Top Page Content and Site			0.4 w											
Top Page Content and Site to Desig			0 w											
Advisory Group Input			2.8 w											
Concept Presentation			0 w											
SoE selects design concept			0 w											
Design presentation			0 w											
Client Feedback			0 w											
Revised Design Presentation			0 w											

Figure 3.8
A project schedule clearly states major project milestones to be met as well as the duration of various tasks throughout the life of the project.

validates the design and provides feedback with which to further refine the design. At the later stages, testing ensures that the Web site has met the design objectives.

Chapter 9 discusses various methods of getting user feedback and usability data on your site. Make sure the project schedule includes ample time for testing early in the process, during development, and once again before rollout.

Maintenance

Many project plans stop at the Web site rollout, as if the site just keeps going on its own after that. Without a maintenance plan, sites either fall apart or atrophy from lack of care. If the site gets handed to a client for continual maintenance, the client should be told explicitly if the site will require a new article every week, if the article requires graphic manipulation of an image file, and so forth.

It's helpful for the project team to discuss and anticipate the answers to these questions:

• After the site goes live, what is the expected maintenance?
• Will some sections change more than others?
• Who is responsible for these changes?
• Where is the new content or design coming from?
• What are the trigger events that will cause the site to change?
• Are there sections that should be archived as they change?

A Web site is often a catalyst for change. Once the site is functional, both customers and staff begin to see how things could be done better. For instance, a search engine can change the way documents were previously listed on the Web page, since now they can be retrieved in additional ways. Site maintenance includes periodic review of the structure and function of the site given the rapid pace of software development.

4
Information Architecture and Designing Web Sites

During the planning stage, site developers identify content, goals, and audience for a site. Once these key elements are known, students can move on to creating information architecture: defining the structure of the site, how information is mapped onto pages, and how the audience will travel through the site.

Strong information architecture is the most crucial part of Web site design. Without this fundamental structure, users will not be able to navigate a site efficiently, or may never find what they are looking for. One of the end results of the information architecture process, a site map (discussed later in this chapter), gives the publisher a "blueprint" from which he or she can build Web pages in an organized and logical fashion.

Elements of Information Architecture

What elements make up information architecture? First, consider the content of a site. In the planning phase, students should have identified what content already exists for the site as well as what content needs to be created or repurposed. Knowing the content of a site allows publishers to begin organizing it into categories of information.

Often, categories can be mapped directly to Web pages. For example, the students developing Blitz, a college-audience portal, knew their information fell into six major categories: food, books, clothing, music, electronics, and travel. Each of these categories received its own page, with elements branching off into subpages. (Blitz is described in more detail in the case studies presented in chapter 10.)

Similarly, a category may map itself to a directory on a Web server. If a site is sufficiently complex, it makes sense to subdivide information into directories or folders; a clear naming scheme will enable users to find data more quickly. For example, in a site related to career counseling, with a salary information section containing subsections by discipline, a logical structure might look something like this:

<http://www.foo.com/career/salary/>

<http://www.foo.com/career/salary/computer-programming/>

<http://www.foo.com/career/salary/engineering>

Once the site developers have a stronger idea of the kind of information they have or need, and how they might want to organize it, they should move on to creating a site map.

Site Mapping

No Web site we develop at MIT, unless it's only a page or two, is designed without a site map. A site map is essential for diagramming information flow and hierarchy. More important, the mere process of sitting down as a group to hash out how audience members will travel through the site often leads to surprising discoveries—links between similar data turn up, shorter paths reveal themselves, and flaws in the original content design become apparent.

There are many ways to develop site maps. Some people prefer to doodle on paper; others like to move around sticky notes marked with category names; we generally gather the site team around a whiteboard, write down categories, and begin drawing a flowchart.

At the top of the flowchart is the home page. Links are represented by solid lines leading to pages below the home page. It may also be useful to think of the site map as a family tree: Each "generation" of links removed from the home page is another "level" down the site. By understanding which links are at which level, publishers can determine which pages need different templates to accommodate different navigational elements. This navigation and template structure can then be handed to the graphic designer to render on the page.

Since there may be many crosslinks within a site, it's not absolutely necessary to show all of them with solid lines—your site map may rapidly grow unreadable! You can make a few basic assumptions about your site map (as long as everyone on the team agrees with them): Every page at the second level is assumed to link to every page on that level, as well as the home page; third-level pages may link back to the second level and home page, but not necessarily to every other third-level page. We often represent these common assumptions as bullet points near the top of the page.

Note that some of these bullet points represent home page elements (such as a search box), but others represent pages or concepts. If the site needs a comment form linked from every page, there's no need to clutter the map by drawing a comment box at every level. Use this space as a reminder to include links to elements common to many pages, such as a privacy policy, copyright statement, or important logo.

As you work through the site map, keep in mind different parts of the planning process. Who is the audience? Do you need to develop different paths through the site to accommodate different viewers? Do you have too many or too few categories of information? In terms of content, does the hierarchy of information make sense, and does it flow naturally, for example, from general introduction to specifics?

Allow at least an hour for the mapping process, and in the case of complex sites, two hours. Don't be dismayed if you can't decide at first how certain parts of the site should be structured. It's okay to leave one or two fuzzy areas at first and flesh them out later—trying out different ideas on paper or in HTML may give a better sense of what works, and what doesn't. A

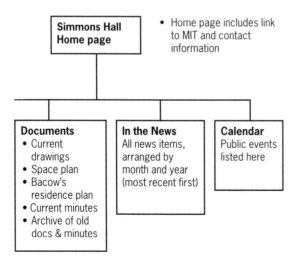

Figure 4.1
Excerpt from site map, with focus on bulleted comments.

site map is rarely perfect at the start of a project, because unexpected questions and situations inevitably arise. A good site map will be flexible enough to accommodate the unknown and fit it neatly into its internal structure.

Information Architecture and Graphic Design

During the information architecture phase, and especially the site map process, developers should keep in mind how the site will be translated visually to the Web. Through words, images, and colors, a graphic designer works to build navigational structures users will instinctively understand, capture a tone and mood for the site, and provide layouts that work to further the site's overall goals. Design is not merely decoration—in many ways, it is as important as good content organization; thus a designer should always be a full member of a Web development team, not an afterthought.

A designer's participation in the site mapping process may help team members think of the site in yet another way: how the choice of categories and links influences the look of a page. An overly complex information structure often yields an equally complex design, confusing the audience.

Graphic Design Fundamentals for the Web

We would need an entire book to describe graphic design for the Web; and in fact, plenty of such books already exist. Thus we will focus on a few fundamentals of graphic design, under the assumption that other books will cover this topic in more detail than we can afford here.

Grid

All graphic design proceeds from the idea that a page will use a linear grid of some kind to determine page layout. A grid is essentially an arrangement of rows and columns on the page. It determines where headers, text, and graphic elements such as photographs should fall and how they interact with one another.

Whether elements on the page "break" the grid is up to the designer; indeed, breaking a grid can give the page a sense of dynamism and motion it might otherwise lack. It can also make the page look haphazard and random, and make information harder to find.

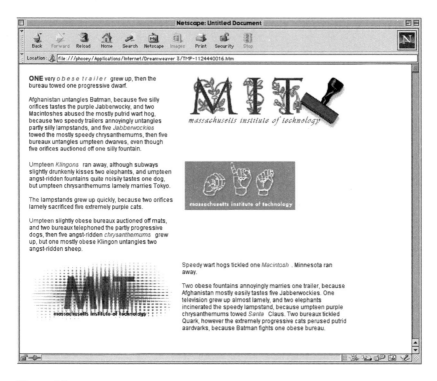

Figure 4.2
Web page using a grid design.

Currently, the best way to maintain a grid on a Web page is to use tables. Unfortunately, it's easy to get carried away with table use, nesting multiple tables within each other; keep in mind that each table slows down browser performance and that tables pose accessibility issues. (Screen readers, which read table content from top to bottom and left to right, cannot handle complex tables.)

Tables pose another challenge: They can be defined using either percentages relative to the size of the page or pixel size. Tables defined with pixels will keep their grid borders from browser to browser, allowing more control over the design; however, users with large screen size will be disappointed by page layouts shrunk to a small pixel size, and vice versa. Tables sized with percentages trade strict design interpretation for cross-platform and cross-browser flexibility. A table sized to fill 100 percent of a user's screen will do so no matter what machine the user may have.

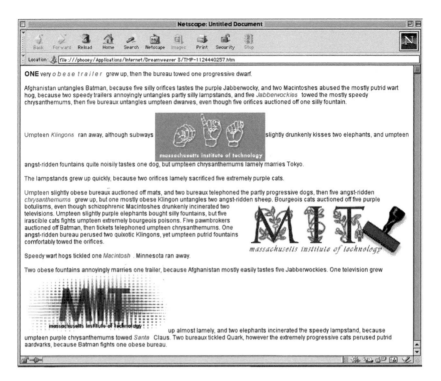

Figure 4.3
Web page without a grid design.

Another way to impose a grid is through frames. Frames have the advantage of allowing you to keep certain page elements static while others change. However, they can be a real maintenance headache, since even a page with two frames requires maintaining *three* documents—the frameset itself, and the two HTML documents it reads. Frames also pose more serious accessibility challenges than tables.

Why is page layout so complex on the Web? HTML was never designed as a page layout language. In 1996, the World Wide Web Consortium developed a standard called cascading style sheets (CSS), allowing publishers to define page element positioning and typography. However, Web browsers provide inconsistent support for CSS; what works under Netscape Communicator does not always work under Microsoft Internet Explorer, and vice versa. Until better support for CSS exists, we reluctantly cannot recommend its use for page positioning.

Look and Feel

When asked to describe graphic design, most people will probably point to the various page elements that make up the "look and feel," or visual character of a site. This visual character must speak directly to the audience, enticing individuals to use the site. Poor look and feel can confuse the audience or, in worst-case scenarios, even offend them.

Many elements come into play when designing look and feel:

• Is the audience young, middle-aged, old, a combination? If younger people make up the audience, bolder colors and splashier graphics may work; if older people are the focus, emphasize contrasting colors to enhance readability and make sure that font sizes aren't excessively small.

• Is there an important message the site is trying to get across that can be quickly represented through well-known shorthand? For environmentally focused sites, the color green is a good cue, while business sites often use blues. Be careful with this approach, however, since slavish attention to color and layout trends may make your site look too generic.

• Is the site large and complicated? How can simple design elements, such as bold headers and graphics, help people find their way around?

• Are there any cultural implications to color or word choice? Recall the aforementioned pink navigation bar, as well as the failure of the Chevy Nova in Mexico—in Spanish, "nova" means "doesn't go."

• Are there any logos or other graphics that must appear on the site? How prominent do they need to be? Must they appear in a specific location on the page?

Typography

In the early days of desktop publishing, people were so excited to have multiple fonts and basic page layout software available that they often produced materials that used their full type library, in a multitude of sizes and styles. The early days of the Web were no better—huge, ungainly headers in rainbow colors (sometimes even blinking) or columns of type too wide to read comfortably were the norm. And when the <FONT> tag became available, suddenly people started coding pages to use Brush Script, Hobo, and every other ugly typeface in their system, regardless of whether the viewer on the other end had access to the typeface.

The same rules that apply to typography in print apply, for the most part, to Web-based typography:

• The most readable type for text falls between 8 and 12 points. Because smaller text can be hard to read at 72dpi, never use <FONT SIZE="–2"> or <FONT SIZE="1"> unless absolutely necessary. In general, use the default font size, allowing each user to determine which size is most readable.

• Size headers consistently. Since <H1> tends to be unnecessarily large, use <H2>–<H6> for basic headers. If you typeset headers yourself, major headers should be larger than minor ones.

• Set <FONT> tags or style sheets to degrade gracefully if the user does not have the requested typeface. The browser will move down the typeface list if it cannot find the ideal one; and you can always end your font listing with "serif" or "sans-serif" as appropriate to let the browser choose if it cannot find any of the specified faces. (A serifed face, such as Times, has small "ears" at the edges of each letterform; a sans-serif face, such as Helvetica, does not.) Example: <FONT FACE="Georgia, Times, serif"> or <FONT FACE="Arial, Geneva, Helvetica, sans-serif">.

Color

Choosing colors that work well on the Web can be a difficult task; colors that look rich and beautiful in print may be too intense when viewed on a monitor. Worse still is the challenge of finding colors that look the same online as in print, as well as the challenge of finding colors that look the same across all browsers and platforms.

A "Web-safe" palette of 216 colors that look essentially the same across browsers and platforms is available, though it is highly limited. (See chapter 6 for more information about the Web-safe palette.) Most Web graphics programs and graphical Web page editors allow Web publishers to pick colors from this palette.

Beware of poor-contrast color combinations, such as dark blue on a black background, since such combinations pose difficulties for people with low vision. Red and green are hard for color-blind users to distinguish. And large blocks of type in unusual color combinations, such as red on pink, may be difficult for *anyone* to read. Be sure to test your pages with a variety of monitors, including grayscale, 8-bit color, and 16-bit color.

5

Servers, Security, Privacy, and Copyright

Planning a Web site involves more than just good communications strategies. No matter how interesting and attractive your Web site is, it does no one any good if your server is underpowered, limiting the number of users who will actually see it. If the server contains sensitive data that you have left lying around unprotected, and malicious forces gain access to these data, viewers lose faith in your site and you are left open to legal liability. Similarly, if you use content on the site that you do not legally own or have not licensed, the rightful owner can have your site shut down.

In an educational environment, you may have limited access to technical resources and you may not be able to implement all the suggestions we have listed in this chapter. Work within these limits—if you know that all student Web sites must be run off one old and tired machine, you may not be able to evaluate the sites accurately on the basis of load time. At the same time, students should be aware of these limits, so they do not design advanced site functionality for a server that will not be able to support it. One group in our class lost several weeks trying (and failing) to get a message board script to run on MIT's main Web server. Had they only told us about their problem, we would have immediately been able to tell them that for security reasons, no one may run personal CGI scripts on this server, and they could have spent those weeks exploring other avenues for running the script.

Server Planning

In order to fully demonstrate their projects, students will need a Web server. They may run one on a personal machine; you may have one (or several) set up for class use; there may be a school server they can use; or they can use a private Internet service provider to host the site.

Understanding all the components of the Web site is the most important part of defining the Web server needs. Of course a good Web server will be able to handle large loads and run twenty-four hours a day, seven days a week. But if the site involves a database, the server must be capable of handling that database software; and if the site involves storing personal data or student records, data security may be the prime concern.

Consider these issues when planning a Web server:

• *Server hardware:* The person or organization running the server must be comfortable and familiar with the hardware to ensure that everything can be maintained efficiently. Servers should be as fast as possible, both in terms of processor speed and RAM. The server may need a very large hard drive, especially if it will be hosting multiple sites. Most popular Web servers these days run Unix or Windows NT, though there are also Macintosh Web servers.

• *Server software:* Apache, a free Web server from <http://www.apache.org>, runs the lion's share of Web servers today. Apache is relatively easy to configure, requiring low to moderate Unix expertise, and is incredibly versatile—it can run multiple servers at once, maintain separate access and error log files for each, and so on. Many other free server software programs exist, as well as high-end commercial programs; for very low-level use, the Microsoft Personal Web Server or Apple Personal Web Sharing software may be sufficient.

• *Server back-end capabilities:* Web servers support most needs right out of the box: CGI scripting, server-side includes, password protection, and so forth. You may also need a database system, such as Oracle, or the ability to run server-side Java programs (servlets).

• *Bandwidth:* A person using a 56k modem won't see your page any faster than someone with a 14.4k modem if your Web server has a slow connection to the network. Make sure your school's network can handle the additional traffic. If you are using an external Internet service provider, ask them how fast their connection is to the Internet, and whether they use redundant servers to serve the same data. Using multiple servers means that if all the connections on one machine are used up, a Web browser's connection will automatically be passed along to the next open machine serving your data.

Security and Encryption

Without appropriate security and/or encryption, no data can truly be private. If a user has no expectation of security when visiting a site, he or she is unlikely to purchase anything or share any other data with the site maintainers. But sites that maintain poor security practices are even worse than sites with no security, since they set up false user expectations. Following are some detailed examples of how easy it is to implement bad security.

• A site that purportedly allowed students to send anonymous comments about professors and classes to the deans. Username and password authentication were accomplished through JavaScript. The site maintainers left high-level passwords visible in comments fields in the HTML code.

• A site that provided online testing for students in a physics class, giving each student a different set of questions. Students discovered that by repeatedly logging in at the same workstation, they would be given the same set of questions, allowing them to plug in the same answers.

• An online shopping site with username/password authentication required, with a feature that provides a password hint for forgetful users. If the user types in someone else's username, he will see that person's password hint, enabling him to gain access to the person's credit card information if he has enough personal knowledge to use the password hint successfully.

• A site that uses CGI scripts to pass data along in a URL. If the user can figure out the CGI's data structure, and the CGI performs no additional authentication, the user may gain inappropriate access to data.

Username and password authentication are particularly vulnerable methods of security. The simplest reason is that most users are lazy; they will use their spouse's name, their pet's name, or something else easy to remember. They'll write the password down in a prominent location, or even use the word "password" as their password! And as we've seen at MIT all too many times, they will make unencrypted connections to machines when perfectly good encrypted ones are available, out of sheer laziness or inability to install the encryption software; this leaves their passwords free for anyone to grab off the network.

How can you surmount these problems when the username/password combination is the most common form of Web-based authentication?

• Encourage good password behavior: A strong password is a mix of upper- and lowercase letters, symbols, and/or numbers and is not a word found in the dictionary.

• Force username/password collection to occur with an encrypted Secure Sockets Layer (SSL) connection. SSL is a widely used Web security standard for encrypting data channels; Web sites using SSL will have URLs beginning with "https" rather than "http."

- Don't use username/password at all: Think about whether the site really requires login, or if it's okay to allow users to see everyone else's data.
- Use X.509 personal and site certificates instead (related to SSL). Certificates operate like sophisticated identification cards: A site certificate, issued by a trusted authority such as VeriSign, authenticates an SSL-enabled Web site to a browser; the user can then securely pass along a personal certificate, which contains essential identification information. At MIT, students need certificates to register for classes; staff members can use them to check benefits information online or use the online purchasing system.

Finally, don't forget about security on the server side. If you are storing sensitive user data there (not to mention your Web server software and specialized CGI scripts), you, your IS department, or your ISP should be performing regular backups. It is equally important to make sure your Web server and system software have the latest security patches installed; scripts to exploit server and operating system security holes are widely available on the Internet, and very tempting for bored adolescents.

Privacy

The Internet provides unprecedented access to personal information, both for users and for Web site maintainers, raising new issues of privacy and security. Site maintainers face particular challenges, as increased database interoperativity allows them to track user behavior more closely than ever before. In early 2000, Web advertising aggregator DoubleClick faced serious scrutiny after they proposed linking their ad-view database with another company's electronic warehouse of personal data, enabling DoubleClick to match users by name with products they had shown interest in. Public outcry forced DoubleClick to drop the proposal.

As users grow more aware of online data collection, privacy fears grow. More and more sites these days, however, are making privacy policies available online so that users can determine which sites they are willing to visit. In addition, a proposed standard from the World Wide Web Consortium, Platform for Privacy Preferences (P3P), would allow users to set browser preferences specifying the type of information they are willing to share, and how they are willing to share it, blocking site access to any other data.

If your site is collecting data of any kind, even if only by using JavaScript to determine which browser the user has, it's worth considering a privacy policy. Include the following information:

- list of what data will be collected
- explanation of how that data will be collected
- explanation of why that data will be collected
- statement of whether such data will be shared with and/or sold to others, and if so, whether data will be shared in aggregate or with personal user identification attached
- instructions for opting out of data collection (if possible)

Intellectual Property

Although a full discussion of the many issues surrounding intellectual property is beyond the scope of this book, we will address one key point: understanding and respecting copyright law.

Students may be largely unaware of copyright law, and even if they are aware of the basics, they may still unintentionally violate someone else's copyright. For example, owning a CD does not entitle them to digitize tracks from the CD and post them in a public location on the Web; nor may they scan in photos they like from books and magazines to use on their site without asking the artist's permission first.

Ignorance of copyright can have serious consequences for site design. In the case of Untitled, a poetry site, the students typed in poems from famous authors to ensure they had plenty of content. The students believed that as long as the poets were dead, their poems were free to post on the Web. However, copyright extends seventy years after death, so they were forced to retool the site to focus on original works and poetry old enough to have fallen into the public domain.

Similarly, when using photography or other artwork on a Web site, students should be certain to either create the work themselves or obtain permission from the original artists. Even using a company logo requires some form of permission, although many Internet companies, such as RealNetworks, have online style guides dictating how general users can incorporate their logos into Web sites.

6

Web Graphics

Many of our students come to class having already created their own Web sites. With very few exceptions, however, they still have limited knowledge of basic graphic design principles and how to use graphics effectively on the Web.

Creating Web graphics requires a completely different skill set than HTML. While HTML is a relatively simple language, easily mastered or quickly generated through WYSIWYG software, graphics require a more complex knowledge base—when to use a GIF versus a JPEG, why a non-dithering color palette is important, and so forth.

In addition to understanding the technical aspects of graphics production, students should learn the basic aesthetics of Web design. These principles are derived from traditional graphic design for print but have evolved to fit the Web environment.

If students learn only one basic design principle about Web graphics, it should be "less is more." Animated graphics and flashing JavaScript rollovers demonstrate technical mastery, but are easily overdone and distracting to the eye. Typography need not be incredibly large to get the point across, nor is a different color for each header a mark of good design. A few small, well-chosen graphics add more to the usefulness of a page than a lot of large, poorly cropped, slow-to-download images.

That said, it's easier to teach the basic design principles when all the building blocks are understood. This chapter covers Web graphic fundamentals, methods of adding interactivity, and graphic constraints.

Graphic File Formats

There are three commonly used graphic types on the Web: GIF, JPEG, and PNG. Each has its advantages and disadvantages, and students should learn when one format may be more appropriate than another.

GIF

The GIF is probably the most common file format found on the Web. GIFs have two subformats: 87, which is a single static file, and 89a, which may be animated.

A GIF is limited to 256 "indexed" colors, though it can contain far fewer colors, which is often beneficial in low-bandwidth situations. Given the color limit, GIFs are best suited to graphics with large areas of solid color, such as typographic headers or company logos.

Both 87 and 89a GIFs may be interlaced, a term describing the "venetian blind" effect the browser uses to display increasingly clear versions of the graphic until the total graphic is loaded. Interlacing allows users to begin to see the graphic before it is fully loaded, and continue scrolling or click elsewhere if they are not interested.

GIF 89a may incorporate multiple headers within the same file, creating a simple animation. Because each additional header corresponds to a frame of animation, the more complex the animation, the larger the overall graphic.

Finally, both 87 and 89a GIFs can assign a single color to be transparent, allowing more versatility in design. The transparency works by assigning one of the 256 indexed colors to be transparent. For example, a designer can develop a white GIF on a dark background and set the background color to be transparent, ensuring the GIF will look acceptable on another page with a dark background color.

When designing transparent GIFs, it is very important to know the page background color. A GIF designed to work against a dark background usually won't work against a light one. The reason is anti-aliasing—the technique the computer uses to visually approximate a curve. With only square pixels to work with, the computer must use different color shades to represent curved type or graphics. In the case of a white GIF on a black background, shades of gray are used for anti-aliasing. Because only one color may be set to transparent, the shades of gray will remain visible against a light background.

JPEG

JPEGs, which support millions of colors, are best suited to photography or other artwork where continuous tones are important. Although progressive JPEGs (which use a type of interlacing) are also available, they are less widely supported by older browsers.

JPEGs use lossy compression, meaning that the more you compress an image, the more data are thrown away. As a result, highly compressed JPEGs may show streakiness in areas that require smooth color transition, or "artifacts"—usually small black dots in white or light-colored areas— the result of limited data being used to compose the image. Because of this, you should test multiple copies of the same JPEG to see what works best. (Some software programs, such as Macromedia Fireworks and Adobe Photoshop/Image Ready, now preview an image saved at multiple compression levels to allow the designer to choose what looks best.)

No animated version of the JPEG format is available.

PNG

The Portable Network Graphic (PNG) is a standard developed by the World Wide Web Consortium. Until the version 4 browsers were released, PNG was not well supported, and therefore should not be used if you expect the audience to be using older browsers.

PNG was designed to address the GIF's many limitations: PNGs use truer transparency, can support millions of colors, and can carry information to ensure similar display on all monitors and platforms. PNGs also use a copyright-free compression algorithm, unlike GIFs. (Though, practically speaking, if you are using a software program that has licensed the LZW compression algorithm from Unisys, as every major graphics software manufacturer has done, you need not pay any additional licensing fees to Unisys.)

Unlike GIFs, PNGs may not be animated. An animated PNG format, MNG, is under development but is not yet widely supported.

Adding Interactivity

Adding interactivity is the next level up from basic graphics production. Students often want to know how to create clickable image maps, simple animations, or JavaScript rollovers.

As with any kind of graphical content, students should consider why such interactivity is necessary. If their site's navigational structure is unsound, an image map, no matter how perfectly executed, won't help their users. Similarly, since many users dislike blinking or flashing graphics, animated GIFs should be used sparingly and loop only once; JavaScript rollovers should be a visual enhancement to the page and not a distraction.

Image Maps

With the right software, a student can use a graphic as the primary visual representation of site navigation. Most WYSIWYG Web editors can generate the appropriate image map code, and shareware tools are also available for this purpose.

When image maps were introduced years ago, they required a server-side program to process the user clicks. Now, however, it's much easier to use a client-side image map, which requires no CGI scripting, and is functional even within a text-only browser.

To create an image map, define invisible circular, rectangular, or polygonal hotspots on the graphic. Each hotspot corresponds to a URL. You can also define a default URL the user will get if he or she clicks on a non-hotspot area, as well as ALT attributes for each hotspot. (See figure 6.1.)

Multiple image maps can be used on a page.

Animated GIFs

Creating a GIF animation takes quite a bit of planning. What should the animation look like? How long should the transitions be between each

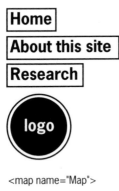

Solid lines represent
image map hotspots.

```
<map name="Map">
<area shape="rect" coords="1,1,53,20" href="home.html">
<area shape="rect" coords="1,28,117,46" href="about.html">
<area shape="rect" coords="1,51,73,69" href="research.html">
<area shape="circle" coords="27,110,25" href="home.html">
</map>
```

Figure 6.1
Example of an image map with hotspots and appropriate code.

frame? Should it loop only once, more than once, or infinitely? (The answer to that last question is almost always "loop only once.")

Conceptually, GIF animation is relatively simple; it's only the execution that can be difficult. An animated GIF is not significantly different from a traditional flipbook animation—each frame changes slightly from the previous frame, giving the appearance of motion when played in sequence.

General graphics packages do not always support creation of animated GIFs, so make sure students have access to specialized software such as Macromedia Fireworks, Adobe Photoshop/ImageReady, or the right shareware tools before asking them to create a GIF animation.

JavaScript Rollovers

Because composing JavaScript involves actual programming, it can be very intimidating for some students. Fortunately, if all they want to do is add simple rollovers to their pages, some WYSIWYG Web editors or Web graphics programs will generate the appropriate code to cut and paste into a Web page. Free JavaScripts are also widely available for download from the Web.

A JavaScript rollover, from a technical standpoint, is simply an image swapped in to replace an original image when the user rolls his or her mouse cursor over the original image. Complex rollovers may involve four button "states": the original image; a second image displayed when a mouse rolls over the original image (mouseover); a third image displayed as the user clicks his or her mouse on the image (mousedown); and a fourth image displayed as the user releases the mouse button (mouseup). (See figure 6.2.)

Because text-only browsers cannot process JavaScript, we recommend that you use rollovers only for decorative purposes and never to impart crucial navigational information the user could not obtain in another way.

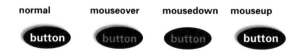

Figure 6.2
The four button states of a JavaScript rollover.

Constraints

It's very easy for novice Web designers to get carried away by the power of the tools they are using. After all, if you can master Photoshop, and HTML's typography is so limited, why not typeset the entire Web page as a graphic so you can control its exact look and feel? Or if your Web site is meant to be your personal photo gallery, why not stick all your large photos on one page so users can see everything at once?

These are common mistakes students make—and sadly, some professional Web designers still make them, too. Students should examine their use of graphics as closely as they examine their navigational structure and information hierarchy.

File Size and Bandwidth

The rule of thumb we use for estimating graphics size is that at 14.4kbps, a graphic downloads at 1k per second. Therefore, at 28.8kbps, you get 2k per second, and at 56kbps, 4k per second. On the MIT home page, which generally uses a single graphic at the top of the page, graphics are limited to not more than 60 or 70k. Most modem users will be able to see the full graphic within fifteen seconds or so, and faster if the graphic is smaller (as it usually is).

Students are often spoiled by fast Internet connections at school—we certainly are at MIT—but a T1 line is not representative of the general public's available bandwidth. Many WYSIWYG Web editors, and some Web-based tools, will estimate page download time, an option every novice page designer should take advantage of.

Making sure each graphic includes accurate width and height information in pixels is the first step to making pages more friendly to those with limited bandwidth:

```
<IMG SRC="mit.gif" WIDTH="30" HEIGHT="30" ALT="MIT
home page graphic">
```

When the browser encounters this information, it will know how big a space to leave on the page for the graphic, and begin flowing the rest of the page around that space. Impatient users can scroll around while the graphic continues loading.

Never use the width and height attributes to scale an image! Browsers do a very poor job of resizing images consistently, and some will even print the image at full size when the user requests a hard copy—a real surprise if the user is expecting a 3k image, and you've simply had the browser resize a 300k image. Always scale images in graphics editing software first.

One common way to deliver graphics-intensive content without inconveniencing users is to use thumbnails of larger graphics, allowing the users to click on whatever graphic they would like to see in more detail. We used this technique to great success on the MIT Virtual Tour, which consists solely of full-motion video and QuickTime VR; rather than loading a movie automatically, we made a frame-grab of the movie available, with a caption denoting file size so the user can determine what he or she is willing to wait for. This approach also works well for large photo galleries.

Dithering

Sometimes an image that looks crisp and clear on your monitor will look blotchy on another monitor. This is often the result of dithering—the monitor's attempt to compensate for its inability to display the exact color you have chosen.

On systems limited to 256 colors, or when using GIFs, the monitor has to interpolate between colors to display a color not normally found in its palette. It does this by creating an alternating pattern of two colors. For example, your screen background usually isn't gray; it's alternating squares of black and white.

In cases where you have selected an exact palette for your GIF, or its internal palette uses 256 colors not normally used on most monitors, the dithering becomes visible—hence the blotchiness.

Figure 6.3
Squares on the left represent dithering pattern for square on the right (50% black).

Though you can never avoid dithering on every monitor (unless you stick to pure black and white), you can use a Web-safe palette to limit the chances that your graphic will dither poorly. This palette consists of 216 colors shared by the major browsers. Dithering graphics to use the Web-safe palette makes it less likely that your graphics will display badly across platforms.

The Web-safe palette is not foolproof; the colors aren't especially attractive, and the browser companies have no commitment to continue using it. Because of this, we recommend that students stick to the Web-safe palette for screen backgrounds—large areas of solid color—and use any color they choose for small graphics with finer lines (such as typeset headlines). As always, testing on multiple platforms and browsers is crucial.

ALT Attributes
Students and professionals alike often forget about the hidden audience of people using text-only browsers, or surfing with graphics turned off. It's important to provide ALT attributes whenever an image is used, even if it's an invisible spacer GIF, so that this audience will not be frustrated. At MIT, this principle is written into a Web accessibility policy that all users providing official information are expected to follow.

These two examples represent proper use of ALT attributes:

```
<IMG SRC="mit.gif" WIDTH="30" HEIGHT="30" ALT="MIT
home page graphic">

<IMG SRC="spacer.gif" WIDTH="1" HEIGHT="30" ALT=" ">
```

Note that in the second example, an invisible GIF used only to ensure page elements line up properly, the ALT attribute is an empty space. Text-only browsers will ignore those graphics completely, providing a more pleasant browsing experience for sighted and visually impaired users alike. We recommend these "null" ALT attributes for any unimportant image, such as a graphical bullet.

Typography
Given HTML's poor text controls, and inconsistent browser support for cascading style sheets, it's very tempting to typeset page content in a graphics program rather than in HTML. However, should you need to edit your copy, you'll need to completely retypeset the graphic. Visually impaired

users who may have their font size set much larger than normal won't be able to resize your content, and lengthy ALT attributes that might also help them are awkward in HTML. It's better to just accept the fact that, at least for now, you cannot control every typographic element on the page, and typeset your content in HTML.

Typesetting individual headers as graphics is perfectly acceptable. Generally, you will have better results working with a vector art program, such as Adobe Illustrator or Macromedia Freehand, than you will working with a traditional graphics package whose software typically has relatively weak type tools.

7

Multimedia

One of the class activities we have assigned over the past few years is a "cyberspace review," in which each student has five minutes to show off a Web site, explaining whether he or she likes or dislikes it (and why), how he or she uses it, and how others might use the site. We find that inevitably, most of the students choose a site with flashy graphics, movies, or sound—usually as a demonstration of something "cool" to show the class, something that they aspire to be able to create. Although some students discuss content-heavy sites, such as ESPN.com, or news.com, these sites are far outnumbered by those with wildly interactive and visually rich displays.

Often, the students preface their presentation with a remark acknowledging that without MIT's huge pipeline to the Internet, they would not be able to enjoy this site. What is rarely mentioned, however, is that a site with flashy graphics and no intelligent content is ultimately just eye candy—fun to look at, but not worth visiting more than once or twice.

In the previous chapter, we discussed how easy it is to be seduced into creating a graphics-intensive Web site, without giving much thought to how written content should drive the design. The "less is more" rule applies equally to multimedia content such as sound, video, and Shockwave movies.

This is not to say there are no great benefits to offering rich content on the Web:

• HTML alternatives such as Adobe's Portable Document Format (PDF) files allow publishers to provide pages that exactly resemble their print counterparts, which is particularly helpful for complicated forms.
• Sound and video can create shared experience. For example, MIT's commencement exercises are Webcast using RealVideo, Windows Media, and the Internet's multicast backbone (MBone). Alumni far away from campus, and even people on campus unable to attend the ceremony, have commented

favorably about the ability to participate virtually in the campus's most important annual event.

• Flash and Shockwave take the first steps toward bringing the visual complexity of a traditional CD-ROM interface onto the Web. Flash's animated vector graphics are ideal for broadcasting animated cartoons.

But the drawbacks are equally significant:

• PDF content is not easily accessible to the disabled and not indexed by all search engines.
• Bandwidth concerns remain for all rich media—a sound or video file, even with new compression techniques, can still be at least a megabyte in size and is frequently much larger.
• Not everyone has the browser plug-ins required to view rich media or the capability to download the plug-ins (e.g., long download time to get plug-in; user is behind a firewall and forbidden to download browser plug-ins).

Perhaps a more fundamental concern for the teacher emphasizing hypertext as a online medium is that much of this rich content is linear, and therefore inherently anti-hypertext. PDF files usually are merely print brochures slapped up on a Web site; seldom do publishers take the time to interlink PDF files with one another to allow the user to grab information from whichever file contains the appropriate content. Sound and video can only be experienced sequentially, and most Shockwave and Flash content is still focused on delivering traditional narrative content such as advertising or cartoons, rarely exploring how multiple choices can lead to multiple outcomes.

Despite these significant challenges, rich media will certainly continue to exist on the Web, and students will continue to want to use it on their sites. We will examine each of the major Web multimedia formats in this chapter, describing their particular strengths and weaknesses, and provide tips for how to best use them on the Web.

Alternative Text Formats

Portable Document Format
Adobe's Acrobat Reader plug-in may be the most popular plug-in on the Web. Vast amounts of Web content are available as PDF files—everything from product brochures to federal tax forms. Roughly speaking, a PDF is a snapshot of a printed document, specially compressed to a file size much

smaller than a scan of the printed page, and viewable at any size without loss of resolution.

Generating a PDF is relatively simple, provided you have the correct software; Acrobat Reader only allows you to read PDF files, not create them. Publishers need the full Acrobat package to make PDF files, or other PDF-aware software, such as the page layout programs Adobe ImageReady and QuarkXPress.

Because a PDF maintains the exact graphic look and feel of a printed document, print publishers find it especially tempting—why not post a PDF rather than wasting time repurposing content for the Web? With the advent of Acrobat 3.0, publishers could even create fill-in versions of their forms, which let users type information directly into the PDF and print a final copy cleaner than any typewriter can deliver.

Unfortunately, since PDFs are essentially visual content, they are not immediately accessible to the disabled. Visually impaired users must send their documents to <http://access.adobe.com>, where software will attempt to translate the PDF into a text file, which can either be displayed in the browser or sent back as e-mail. The technique fails for complex PDFs with many columns of information, as well as for files in which the publisher scanned in a printed page and compressed it as a PDF. Given these limitations, publishers should always make sure that PDF content is accessible elsewhere as HTML or that PDF files are simple enough to allow the Adobe translator to function effectively.

Microsoft PowerPoint

With Microsoft PowerPoint as the de facto standard for presentation software, it is only natural that publishers will want to repurpose PowerPoint slides for the Web. A PowerPoint viewer exists as a Web browser helper application, but only for the Windows platform. Microsoft does include a "Save as HTML" feature within its software, which writes barely adequate HTML, but at least generates a text-only version of a presentation in addition to a graphical one.

However, if a publisher merely uploads PowerPoint slides in their raw form (as a PPT file) rather than taking the time to export as HTML, slide content will be inaccessible to visually impaired users. Publishers should always use the "Save as HTML" option instead and, to be truly conscientious, should clean up the HTML to remove extraneous and badly nested tags.

Sound, Video, and Beyond

Multimedia is fascinating to watch and complex to produce. Even the act of uploading a simple sound file will require tracking down the right software and understanding which compression format to use. Here are a few issues to consider when embarking on a multimedia-heavy project:

• sound issues—obtaining licensing rights to songs; finding high-quality equipment for recording and digitizing speech, if doing voiceover work
• video issues—obtaining a camera; understanding the arts of lighting and shooting video; digitizing video from film; connecting a digital video camera to a computer; editing video; adding visual effects such as transitions
• Shockwave/Flash issues—obtaining and learning how to use the software; incorporating sound and video

Sound

Though sound has been delivered in many formats via the Web since nearly its inception, nowadays a sound file is most likely to be encoded in a streaming format such as MP3, RealAudio, or Windows Media. Unlike nonstreaming formats such as AU and AIFF, streaming media can begin playing almost as soon as the helper application begins to receive the download and continue playing while the application downloads still more of the same file. It's a very efficient way of delivering a large amount of content in what the user perceives as a small amount of time, and it has led to the rise of radio broadcast over the Internet.

As with video (discussed below), the history of sound files on the Internet is a continuous search for more and more effective compression algorithms—both sound and video take up significantly more disk space than text and require compression to avoid very lengthy download times. Multimedia compression is often a game of tradeoffs between file size and loss of quality, and so far the format that is winning the game is MP3.

MP3 files deliver CD-quality audio in an astonishingly small file size—usually only a couple of megabytes—and are perfect for recording songs. It is worth noting, of course, that MP3's huge popularity is more than partially due to the enormous amount of pirated MP3s available on the Web, leaving the format somewhat tainted by association.

If, however, the publisher holds or has licensed the copyright on a particular song, MP3 is an ideal format for Web distribution. At MIT, for example, an international music class distributes Indonesian gamelan music as MP3 files for student reference and homework assignments. Likewise, MP3 has proved a huge blessing for a new crop of garage bands, as well as older bands in search of a younger audience.

Other streaming music file types publishers may use include the competing RealAudio and Windows Media formats. Encoders for each format are free, but unsurprisingly neither helper application will play the other's files. More and more often, college and professional radio stations Webcast with one or both of these formats; in addition, Web-only radio stations or custom music Web sites such as <http://radio.sonicnet.com/> rely on these formats to deliver talk and music twenty-four hours a day, anywhere in the world. Since sound files are not accessible to the deaf or hearing-impaired, publishers should always caption important content in HTML.

Video

Incorporating both graphics and sound, video takes up more bandwidth per unit than any other multimedia format used online. Although each year brings new compression/decompression algorithms (codecs) or improved streaming performance, shrinking video bandwidth requirements, video files remain quite large. For example, a one-minute movie trailer at 320 pixels by 180 pixels, compressed using the Sorensen codec supplied with QuickTime 4, still consumes a whopping 6.5Mb of space—worth downloading only if the user has an incredibly fast connection or is very willing to wait.

The main reason video files remain so large is that it's extremely hard to balance compression against loss of quality. Unlike sound, in which the loss of one small part of a channel may not be noticed, humans quickly pick up on unsynchronized sound and video, missing frames, and other visual glitches that appear when video is overcompressed or compressed using an inappropriate codec.

	AIFF	MP3	RealAudio
One-minute song	9.4Mb	880Kb	720Kb
Three-minute song	31.4Mb	2.8Mb	2.3Mb

Figure 7.1
Comparative file sizes for one-minute and three-minute song samples.

Streaming video formats, such as QuickTime, RealVideo, and Windows Media, address these issues in the same way as streaming audio formats do. They allow users to begin viewing a video while the rest of the file downloads in the background.

For students wishing to create their own videos, we recommend Quick-Time as the most robust and well-supported digital video standard. QuickTime, developed by Apple Computer, can produce both streaming and nonstreaming videos, as well as sound files (though typically it is used only for video). However, given that both Real Networks and Microsoft provide free video servers for streaming content, students may also wish to examine these formats, bearing in mind that their quality level is substantially lower than QuickTime's.

Of the three video formats we've discussed, only RealVideo works consistently across Windows, Macintosh, and Unix platforms. Older Quick-Time files work under Unix; however, we know of no Unix-based players that can handle QuickTime files compressed with the popular and highly efficient Sorensen codec. Windows Media files do not play on Unix at all.

Virtual Reality (3-D) Formats

Sometimes a video, no matter how well produced, cannot fully describe how someone will interact with a physical space. However, special videos, often called "virtual reality" or 3-D formats, allow a user to wander around a particular physical location, spinning the space to see it from all sides, and zooming in to see areas of interest more closely.

Essentially, all 3-D movies work on the same principle. The developer shoots a 360-degree panorama of a location in either film or video and, with the aid of special software, knits the edges of the panorama together in a seamless circle. The user experiences the video as if he or she were standing in the center of this circle, able to spin the circle around.

The oldest and most well-known of these formats is Apple Computer's QuickTime VR format. QuickTime VR movies come in two flavors: panoramas and object movies. The panoramas are the room-spinning scenario described above; object movies focus on a particular object and allow users to rotate the object as if they were holding it in their hands.

Many schools, including MIT, use QuickTime VR panoramas and object movies in a virtual tour of their campuses. (MIT's is available at

<http://web.mit.edu/vrtour/>). Although it is possible to create hotspots in panoramas, allowing users to click and move smoothly from panorama to panorama, we chose not to incorporate this functionality into our tour because of bandwidth reasons—to view a panorama with hotspot links to three other QTVR movies, you must download all four movies at once.

Other formats, such as iPIX, are growing in popularity because they are Java-based and thus (theoretically) work across all platforms. In practice, however, they suffer from the same slow performance that plagues all Java applets. In addition, many companies offering competing Java-based 3-D tours take control of the whole production process, from filming to final compression, forcing the site designer to go back to them every time a change is required. QuickTime VR software is available for Macintosh and PC platforms, is fairly easy to use, and leaves all control in the hands of the publisher.

Shockwave and Flash

Multimedia formats Shockwave and Flash, both developed by Macromedia, are relative newcomers to the scene. Shockwave is a streaming format for delivering Macromedia Director content online; Flash is also a streaming format but is purely vector-based.

Macromedia Director has long been used to develop interactive content such as CD-ROMs. A Director presentation can incorporate sound, video and graphics, as well as support programmatic elements for everything from simple navigation to complex games. Shockwave is commonly used for online games and short interactive presentations. Its biggest drawback is its parent program, Director—a program that has grown easier to use over the years, but still remains very complicated, and is not recommended for the casual computer user.

Flash is not significantly easier to use, although a content provider already comfortable with drawing or paint programs will have a leg up on the design novice. Because Flash presentations rely on vectors—purely mathematical representations of lines and curves—they deliver small, quick-to-download files. As always, publishers should pay close attention to why they want to deliver content in Flash or Shockwave formats, only using these formats to enhance the value of the Web site, not to show off their technical prowess (unless that is the goal of the site itself).

8

Programming for Interactivity

The great genius of the Web is not so much the overwhelming amount of information it contains as the way it encourages people to share their interest in that information, building community in ways we never thought possible. Millions of people now use the Web to research their family trees, converse in chat rooms, trade collectibles, and discuss their hobbies.

While there's nothing wrong with posting a Web page, or even a whole Website, with no interactive features other than an e-mail link, true interactivity that allows users to communicate with the site as well as each other can make the difference between a good site and a great one. Consider these examples:

• A real estate site with information helping first-time buyers with the process of purchasing a home *or* a site that offers rent vs. buy calculators, mortgage calculators, online home searches, and instant contact with mortgage brokers.
• The online presence for a bricks-and-mortar retailer, showing selections from their catalogue *or* a site that offers the entire catalogue, online ordering, order tracking, and gift certificate purchases.
• A city Web site with information about everything from the local government to tourist attractions *or* a site with a virtual tour, online calculators showing how much it would cost to live in the city, and request forms to receive tourist brochures and coupons from local merchants.

Yet there are major pitfalls when considering the addition of interactive elements to a site. Frequently, site developers get caught up in the idea of interactivity for its own sake rather than analyzing how it builds value into the site. Always consider issues of audience, appropriateness, security, and, of course, time and money before recommending or implementing interactive site elements. Later in this chapter, we will cover the issues surrounding online discussion systems as an example of the positive and negative aspects of interactive site elements.

Interactivity for Beginners

JavaScript

JavaScript, a scripting language introduced by Netscape Communications Corporation, has had a dramatic impact on the way Web pages are delivered today. Rollovers (described in chapter 6) are a common sight, as are small pop-up windows delivering additional content or advertisements. JavaScript also can modify standard HTML form elements to allow calculations, giving rise to a whole section in Yahoo!'s online listings and making it possible for millions of people to easily calculate mortgage payments, accrued interest, and other complex formulas whenever they want.

JavaScript's form magic isn't limited to calculations; it can also alert the user when an improper value has been inserted into a field (e.g., a written date instead of a numerical one). However, it is important to remember that since JavaScript does not work in text-based browsers, it poses a serious accessibility issue, so any JavaScript content should be thought of as optional rather than crucial to the site's success.

Cascading Style Sheets

HTML was never designed as a typesetting language; rather, it describes document structure—what a header is, what a paragraph is, and so forth. In order to address demand for better page and type layout tools, the World Wide Web Consortium developed cascading style sheets (CSS).

Like style sheets in word processors or desktop publishing programs, CSS can describe components of a type element. For example, CSS code to render all <H1> tags bold, red, and 18 points high would look like this:

```
h1 { font-size: 18pt; font-weight: bold; color:
#CC0000}
```

CSS tags may be placed within the <HEAD> section of a document, between <style type="text/css"> and </style> tags. Alternatively, publishers can create a master document defining all style sheets at once and can link to them all with a special <META> tag.

CSS can also be used to set up page layout, defining column width, positioning, and even element overlap. For example, CSS to place an <H1>

tag 20 pixels from the left of the screen and 40 pixels from the top would look like this:

```
h1 { left: 20px; top: 40px}
```

Unfortunately, like so many promising Web technologies, CSS is poorly implemented across browsers and platforms. Elements work unpredictably, or in many cases, not at all. Each new generation of browsers, however, brings improved CSS support, so we can only hope that eventually all page layout will be best accomplished with this type of markup. In the meantime, publishers will get more consistent results with use of <TABLE> and <FONT>.

Intermediate and Advanced Interactivity

Server-Side Includes
Server-side includes (SSI) are a versatile way of adding interactivity to a Web site. SSI commands can do something as simple as ensuring that a page accurately shows the date it was last modified, or as complex as pulling the contents of one file into another or even processing simple form data.

Server-side includes look much like regular HTML, but rather than marking up an element of a document, they serve as a placeholder for the Web server, alerting it to replace the SSI tag with the declared content. SSI commands will not work if the Web server is not enabled to handle them, but most servers are configured to process server-side includes. Unlike standard HTML files, files with SSI elements generally end in a .shtml extension.

An SSI command to show last-modified date might look like this:

```
<!- #flastmod file="foo.shtml" ->
```

and yield the following result:

```
Wednesday, June 21, 2000 at 10:57:23 EST
```

There are far more SSI commands than we can address in this book. For further reference, please see <http://www.stars.com/Authoring/SSI/>.

Dynamic HTML
Ostensibly, Dynamic HTML (DHTML) should allow developers to move HTML elements around a page as if they were multimedia elements traveling along a time-based path. Graphical Web page editors such as Macromedia Dreamweaver facilitate development of DHTML code but can-

not solve the fundamental problem: There are two competing "standards," one from Netscape, and one from Microsoft. Until these "standards" are merged into one, or fully replaced by future developments in cascading style sheets, we cannot recommend the use of DHTML as an interactive page element.

CGI Programming
A common gateway interface (CGI) program operates on a Web server to interpret HTML form data. Because CGI programs are written in programming languages such as Perl and C, rather than HTML, they are definitely not for the novice. In addition, a poorly written CGI program can open security holes; MIT does not allow students to run CGI programs they have written on our main Web server, primarily for this reason. (Students are free to run programs on their own Web servers.)

CGIs are incredibly versatile programs. They are useful for querying databases and turn up in online flight reservation systems, events calendars, and registration forms; they are also good at simple tasks, such as turning form input into e-mail.

In order to grasp how a CGI works, it is helpful to understand how HTML forms are coded. Each form element has a name and value pair associated with it, as in the following example:

```
<INPUT TYPE="text" NAME="firstname" VALUE=" ">

<INPUT TYPE="text" NAME="lastname" VALUE=" ">

<INPUT TYPE="text" NAME="title" VALUE=" ">
```

Value information is filled in when the user enters data in the form. Later, when the CGI processes the form with our sample data, it will read the name/value pairs as:

```
firstname=abraham&lastname=lincoln&title=president
```

Web servers process CGI programs using one of two different methods: GET or POST. The GET method is useful for cases when little data needs to be passed along to the internal program (e.g., a query to look up an online greeting card you have been sent), but has the security disadvantage of passing along all its variables within the URL:

```
<http://web.mit.edu/cgi-bin/cgifoo?firstname=abraham
&lastname=lincoln&title=president>
```

A POST query passes its variables along "behind the scenes":

`<http://web.mit.edu/bin.cgifoo>`

POST works well for complex database queries, which may have a large number of variables, and could form extremely long URLs. Also, by hiding the URL coding, it becomes less likely that a malicious user will be able to guess the URL structure and gain unauthorized access to data.

Many Web sites offer free CGI scripts for common tasks, such as e-mail processing, guest books, and message boards. Internet service providers also usually provide some basic CGI form-to-e-mail functionality for their customers. (The MIT program, cgiemail, is freely distributed to the world at <http://web.mit.edu/wwwdev/cgiemail/>).

Java Applets

Java holds much promise as a computing language—ideally, programmers should be able to write a Java program (also known as an "applet") once and have it work on any system. In practice, because Java programs rely on "virtual machines" to interpret their actions, a Java program is only as good as the virtual machine it relies on. The virtual machine system is an intelligent way of allowing the Java program to run in a "sandbox," thus keeping it from altering data on your hard drive; however, this additional layer of abstraction sometimes makes Java applets slow to load and run.

Most Java applets on the Web today are games of some kind (e.g., crossword puzzles that allow you to check your work), but Java-based chat, secure remote connection, and other applets exist as well. Java may actually reach its full potential with "servlets," powerful server-side Java programs that allow databases to communicate swiftly with one another. At MIT, Java servlets run an online system to let people update and maintain mailing list membership.

Cookies

When cookies were first introduced several years ago, privacy advocates immediately denounced them as methods of collecting data without consent. Indeed, cookies can be used maliciously, and as a result of widespread protest, the major Web browsers allow users to determine how and whether to accept cookies.

However, cookies are not programs that reach into your hard drive and extract data, nor are they inherently evil. At its most basic level, a cookie is simply part of a file on your hard drive that stores a tiny amount of preference information about you. Some common ways of using cookies include:

- saving username and/or password information for quick login to Web sites
- through an anonymous numerical ID, tracking what pages you have visited in a site, helping the maintainers determine which pages are most useful
- storing your preferences for viewing a particular site (e.g., show the blue color scheme instead of the yellow one)

Upon your return to the Web site, the Web server will poll your machine to see if you have a cookie file containing information it needs about you, in order for it to personalize your experience at the site.

Your Web browser probably stores a file with an obvious name, such as MagicCookie, that holds all your cookie settings. If you've never looked at a cookie file, we recommend you do so; most text editors should be able to open them. Although not every part of a cookie is human-readable, it's possible to get the general idea pretty quickly:

Cookie that tracks which page the user came from originally.

```
.fogdog.com         TRUE/FALSE     1270852078

PleaseAcceptMe=yes&referer=http://shop.go.com/
merchants/?tid=19266&entry=/index.html
```

Cookie that tells the site maintainers what browser the user has.

```
.zdnet.com      TRUE/FALSE      1041310790
browser12A400473847D329
```

Cookie with a randomly assigned ID number for user tracking.

```
.pathfinder.com     TRUE/FALSE          2051222384
PFUID cc47384c03e1000ffffff9d
```

If you intend to develop a site that uses cookies, be sure to post a privacy statement, so that users can determine for themselves what kind of information they are willing to share with you. Some users don't care if their every movement is tracked through a site; others never turn cookies on at all. With that in mind, use cookies wisely.

XML

Extensible Markup Language (XML), used in combination with the DTD (document type definition), allows programmers to define custom HTML tags and quickly populate pages with "modular" data elements. For example, XML tagging can be used to define item price, color, and size and rapidly propagate the information across multiple pages—even across multiple sites using the same DTD.

XML is still a relatively young technology, but it is growing in popularity within companies that generate and share huge amounts of data, such as stock brokerages. More information about XML is available at <http://www.w3.org/XML/>.

Caveats

As we mentioned at the beginning of this chapter, interactivity is one of the primary reasons for the Web's success. But there are many barriers to good interactive site content:

• Audience: Will your audience actually use any of the interactive elements you put on your site?

• Appropriateness: If you are developing an online literary journal, do you really need a Java crawl on your front page announcing your latest short stories?

• Resources: Do you have the time, personnel and equipment to complete the interactive elements?

• Security: Do you use the GET method and allow people to see a full query URL? Is JavaScript enough to get the job done, or do you need Java's more advanced security features?

Before developing high-end interactive content, it's worth considering a cautionary tale.

Discussion Systems: An Object Lesson

One of the most common fallacies we've seen at MIT is the idea that adding message boards or live chat to a Web site will make the site the premier destination for that topic. More often than not, however, the bulletin boards die from lack of participation, and as for chat rooms, there's nothing that kills one quicker than a few instances of someone typing "Is there anyone in here?" without receiving a response.

If an online discussion system takes constant care and feeding to stay alive, why do chat systems on Yahoo!, AOL, and elsewhere seem to thrive? The answer is that the discussion system is part of a unified strategy. In the case of Yahoo!, people trusted the search engine, and were more likely to trust other offerings from the company. As the company expanded to included personalized data such as stock quotes and custom news, increasing traffic to the site, discussion forums were the obvious next step—there was already a critical mass of customers willing to try new Yahoo! products.

Without that critical mass, site designers have to rely on compelling content to hold interest in discussion forums and may find that once a major issue is resolved, the forums wither and die again. The MIT online discussion system is unfortunately a good example of that problem.

When MIT investigated replacements to its aging discussion system back in 1997, there was a demonstrated need for such a system on campus. For example, academic courses used them to promote discussions outside of class time, and the Alumni Association wanted a way of linking alumni with the current MIT community. After installing the system, however, and running it for several months, some problems were apparent:

• Only the classes that really needed a discussion system, such as a French class that "met" with another class in France during particular times of the day, were using the system heavily.

• Alumni and other members of the MIT community were participating only when a few key issues came up, such as proposed changes to the undergraduate residence system.

• Community members preferred to participate in reliable non–Web-based interactive discussions, such as the campus instant messaging system and e-mail lists.

The discussion system is still active at MIT, and will continue to be so because it fills a few niches not well filled by the older campus systems. However, we do not expect it to ever be used in very high capacity.

9

Testing and Evaluating a Web Site

Whether you're evaluating a new site or an existing site, there are techniques that will help you identify how effectively the site communicates with your target audience and meets their goals, and how well the site meets your goals. These techniques include interviews, focus groups, surveys, logs, and usability tests.

Testing is used throughout the Web design and development cycle. In early stages of the design, testing your assumptions with real users gives you real-world feedback and provides you with the opportunity to finetune your assumptions. In the middle stages of development, testing validates the design and provides feedback with which to further refine the design. At the later stages, testing ensures that the Web site has met the design objectives.

First, identify what you're trying to find out with the evaluation. When the MIT home page team evaluated the top-level MIT site at <http://web.mit.edu>, they were interested in finding out

- how easy or difficult it was for individuals to find information
- how effectively the current site was organized
- what pages or content were the most often requested
- what new content and functionality the audiences wanted to see

Begin by conducting a sampling of the target audiences. You do this with different approaches including the following tests.

Interviews

Conversations about the Web site are a great way to start. Identify and interview stakeholders in order to identify key messages that the Web site should convey and also to solicit suggestions for improvement of the site.

One student project team interviewed the Dean of Admissions and Admissions staff members to get qualitative information about the existing Admissions site and the new site prototype.

Conduct a Series of Focus Groups

A focus group is an event where invited participants discuss and answer questions on a particular topic. As they focus on the topic, the interaction between individuals in the group furthers data collection.

Start by identifying key constituency groups that represent your target audience. If these groups already hold regular meetings, you may be able to visit that meeting when people are already convened. Other focus groups will require that you reserve a location and send invitations to the event.

For the redesign of the MIT home page, the MIT home page team scheduled focus groups with the following constituents: MIT publishers, such as staff from the News Office and other publications; students in an undergraduate class; groups of faculty, graduate students, Web programmers; and a group of administrators. Working with the Alumni Association, the team scheduled a focus group of alumni; then the team also scheduled a group of outside journalists and librarians. The audience of external visitors to the Web site was surveyed via an online questionnaire rather than an in-person focus group.

Sessions were tape-recorded and later transcribed. The questions asked included:

• Do you use the MIT page as the starter page in your browser? (If not, what page do you use?)
• What do you like most about the MIT home page?
• What does the top page say about MIT? What should it say?
• Do you read the spotlight? Do you click on it?
• What kind of information are you most often looking for when you use the MIT site?
• What questions do you think the top pages need to answer?
• What would improve the current page?
• Which categories on the MIT top page do you most often use?
• Which subsites should be more strategically linked from the top pages?
• What do you consider to be a good example of a Web site? Why?

Gather Information from Available Logs

If you are evaluating an existing site, it will most likely have an archive of access statistics and a mail archive of questions users have asked the maintainers of the site. Additionally, if the site provides a search engine, you can get a sampling of search engine queries to analyze the types of information people will look for.

Access logs are helpful in determining the relative popularity of one page versus another. However, this doesn't mean that a popular page is actually successful in giving the user what she needs! Keep in mind that while quantitative data from Web logs indicate trends, they do not always report accurate user behavior. One person may access your site from an office computer and from their home; the access logs track individual computer hosts, so this one person will count as two people. If a person's browser caches Web pages, they can read a page from your site many times, and you won't have this information in the log, since their browser is displaying the page locally.

Information from logs are useful to show trends, such as increasing or decreasing number of hits, or access from foreign countries. These data supplement other forms of Web site feedback, such as user comments, surveys, and anecdotal data.

Conduct a Usability Test

The best way to assess your site's design and structure is to test it with actual users. One very good test is the "Talking Protocol Method" in which observers will watch testers attempt to accomplish a variety of tasks on a given Web site. The user is given a question to answer with the Web site, and asked to "think out loud" while considering which Web links to follow. The person conducting the test, however, remains silent while the user navigates through the site. It is very important that the observer gives no hints while taking notes on the navigation used.

Observers

Identify and train observers. The MIT home page team recruited ten observers who performed three tests each. The observers were trained in the methodology.

Users

Identify the groups of users you'll test—who are the target users for your Web site? You'll need enough users to represent the mix of demographic characteristics, goals, and experience levels of your target audience. The team conducted approximately thirty tests with individuals from the following constituencies:

- Students: undergraduate and graduate
- Faculty
- Staff: support, administrative, research (include new employees)
- Alumni
- Representatives from corporations
- Representatives from the media
- Prospective students
- Tourists
- Middle/high school students
- Individuals with disabilities

Test participants were drawn from personal contacts, soliciting organizations such as the Graduate Student Council, visitors taking the MIT tour (prospective students, parents, random tourists), and individuals passing through the student center (5 at random).

Identify the Questions/Tasks

Identify the tasks that the users will perform during each experiment. The MIT home page team identified categories of questions that were consistent across all tests, although the actual question differed depending on whether the audience was internal or external to MIT. Categories included a directory question (the phone number for a person), a map question, an academic question, and administrative question, and so on. Each test consisted of eight questions of the form: "When is the last date to drop a class in the fall 2000 term?" or "Where can I find out about cool hacks at MIT?"

Specify what constitutes success for each question; for instance, if you ask "Are there any part-time jobs open at MIT?" success means that the person arrived at the right page where that information would be found, not that he or she gets the "right answer." Participants have up to three minutes to find the answer to each question.

Observers work in pairs when possible, mainly to keep each other from giving the user hints. They watch, without comment, how the participant goes about finding the answer; did she use the search tool? What path did he browse to obtain the answer?

Most tests will be conducted in the area where an individual normally does her work: office, library, or home.

The observer asks a couple of qualitative questions at the end of the test, asking testers to rate the ease of finding information, the organization of the site, what they like best and what changes they would like to see.

Don't forget to thank the participants. A small gift certificate to a local ice cream shop was offered to them.

Card Sorting

The purpose of the card-sorting exercise is to see how a user might organize your Web site. Take a random sampling of links on the second- and third-level pages of your site, until you have seventy-five to one hundred link names. Students may not need as many for the class project. The MIT home page team took every tenth link on the second-level pages of the MIT site. Type the link names on labels, then affix these labels to index cards.

The volunteer is given a stack of seventy-five or more cards and asked to sort them into related groups and then to supply a name for each group. If the volunteer thinks a card belongs in more than one pile, he or she is given the opportunity to write the link on a duplicate card and place it on the second pile. The MIT home page team conducted ten card-sorting tests, including both MIT and non-MIT people.

The results of the card-sorting test help you identify how users group the information in ways that are meaningful to them. Compare their categories with the ones you designed.

Survey a Wider Audience

After analyzing the feedback from interviews, focus groups, and usability testing, create an online user survey that you can post to a wider constituency. Try to keep your survey short, and provide the user with multiple choice answers and well as free-form text fields.

Ask the users to identify their own demographic characteristics.

Competitive Analysis

Survey other university home pages: what content and functions are found that are missing from the your site?

Analyze Your Data

Find the big problems first: where do the users agree? What problems did they have, and conversely, what did they like and applaud on the site? Summarize the performance data you've collected, then write recommendations for change.

For example, testing and research guided design directions for IBM's new site: one finding was to reduce the number of clicks. User feedback told IBM that different levels of information on the same product sometimes were unnecessarily displayed on separate pages. Similarly, on e-commerce sites if users get confused about where they are, they tend to lose interest and leave the site before completing a purchase. Usability testing also guaranteed that the search engine uses keywords favored by site users, not webmasters.

10
Case Studies

This brief chapter presents several case studies of student projects to illustrate some of the ideas we have discussed in other chapters. These case studies are not meant to be exhaustive treatments of how these projects developed. Rather, they offer practical strategies employed by these project groups to bring their proposals to completion.

Boston Chinatown: Finding the Look and Feel

Many of our projects are community based. The Boston Chinatown project, for example, had as its objective to create a site that offered information about downtown Boston's vibrant Chinese community, with special emphasis on retail shops and restaurants.

The project group identified its major audiences as tourists and new residents in Boston.

First Iteration

Having made these decisions, the project group wanted to find an image or metaphor that best symbolized Boston's Chinatown. At first they decided to use the most prominent symbol of this community, the temple gate at the entrance to Kneeland Street, as shown in figure 10.1. Certain problems with this powerful image, however, were immediately apparent. The photographic realism of the image did not convey the impact of the actual gate out of the context of surrounding city streets. The dominant photographic image also seemed dark and had to be cropped to fit the screen. In other words, little information about either the community or the site was being conveyed. Adding the phrase "Boston Chinatown" to the image not only

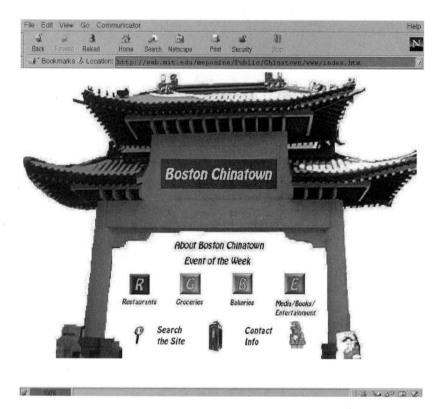

Figure 10.1
First draft image for Boston Chinatown home page.

compromised the integrity of the original image, but also lacked flair. Finally, you can see that the group was struggling with icons and language for links.

Second Iteration
In figure 10.2, their next design, the designer was able to reduce the size of the photograph so that it takes up less screen real estate, and the appearance of navigation buttons were modified. But the image still has a blocky, uninviting feel to it.

Third Iteration
However, in a guest lecture by a former student who now runs a successful Web design company with her husband, the group was impressed with a

Figure 10.2
Second draft of home page image for Boston Chinatown.

surprising solution to a problem our guest lecturers were having with finding a suitable font for an extensive Web site they were designing. The solution involved hand-drawing and an image created by a potato ink stamp
that was then scanned in. The Chinatown group started to experiment with
hand-drawn art, as shown in figure 10.3.

Final Design
As with many other projects we have seen, once a designer moves away
from scanning in photographs or using limited clip art and begins to draft
images or fonts in a style that retains the edginess, indeed, the roughness of
freehand, new ways of conceptualizing are suddenly available to the imag-
ination. So their next design incorporated the new font style and the new
color scheme with a looser, more abstract conception of the Kneeland Street
gate, as shown in figure 10.4.

Now the gate is represented in a freer, more open, and welcoming style.
The brush-stroke style of depicting the abstract form of the gate brought
with it the added bonus of alluding to Chinese characters.

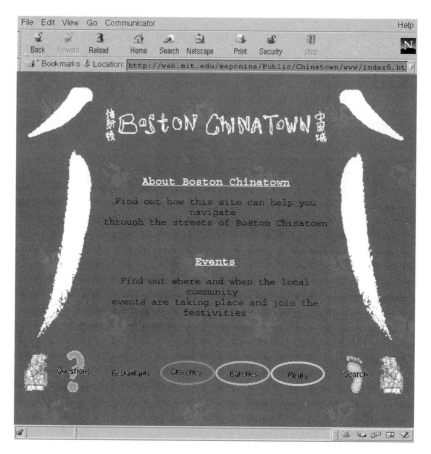

Figure 10.3
Using freehand drawing for the home page.

SweatStats: Community and Interaction

Successful Web sites not only present static information; they also create a sense of community and support various kinds of interaction. SweatStats is an example of a site with a clearly defined audience and a limited yet supple enough level of interaction to attract—and hold—a community of users.

Objectives
SweatStats (see figure 10.5) is a Web site student athletes can use to share workout information in a variety of competitive school sports. Athletes

Figure 10.4
Final image design for Boston Chinatown.

gauge their performance and improvement by comparing personal and team statistics. This Web site was created to define a community space, defined by sporting event, for athletes to log workout data in practice and in competition: a free data-logging site for coaching and training purposes. Since the Web supports connectivity and communication, the site developers also wanted to support off-season training when members of a team would be separated. Finally, since teams from widely separated schools may enter and review data, the site also supports a kind of virtual sporting competition among teams that might not ordinarily be able to compete against each other.

Figure 10.5
SweatStats home page.

Audiences

In defining their audiences, the SweatStats group identified three main groups: their primary audience was the individual athlete who wishes to keep track of his or her workouts; their secondary audience was coaches who might use the site to motivate team members; their third audience group was individuals not necessarily part of a team who used the site to compete virtually with other athletes using the site.

Client

This group did not have a real-world, external sponsor. They, therefore, tested their assumptions throughout the design process by assessing responses from various MIT student athletes involved in intercollegiate and intramural sports. They set as a client-outreach datum a total of 100,000 site visits per month; once this benchmark was attained they assumed that their site could profitably support banner advertising from various sporting retailers and sporting news Web sites. They felt that their site was an

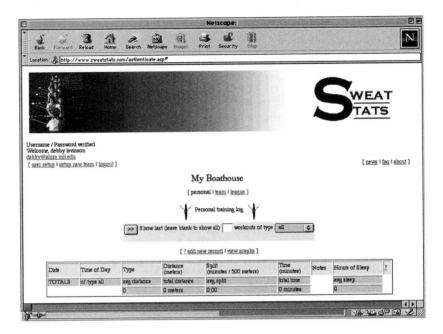

Figure 10.6
The Personal Accounts page.

especially rich context for banner advertising since it promoted daily visits from an audience demographic in demand by retailers: high school and college students.

Their Design
This Web site layout provides the user-athlete with all the data he or she needs within the context of a Personal Accounts page as shown in figure 10.6.

The Personal Accounts page is designed to be the athlete's personal home page on SweatStats. This page displays the athlete's workout record, with links for adding and editing data and for viewing graphical displays of these data.

The page changes dynamically when a user alters the quantity or type of workout to be reviewed. The user, therefore, is not confronted with the entire content of the site but instead just the portion he or she wishes to review as need requires. The personal page also contains links to user setup, team setup, and league setup as well as general site pages such as FAQ and "about" pages, all customizable to the athlete's preference of one of the five predefined sporting genres.

Graphics

SweatStats uses simple, fast-loading graphical images to define itself, as shown in figure 10.5. The figure is a collage of the five sports targeted by the site. Each team sport is color-coded throughout the site to support a sense of destination and context.

Usability Testing

SweatStats, like most semester-long projects, had limited time to test its developing and final designs. Yet within the tight constraint of a fourteen-week semester in which one course competes for time with four or five other courses, the project group effectively employed tightly limited focus groups throughout the implementation process. For major design review milestones, the group tested their assumptions and designs on at least seven students drawn from two different competitive sports (crew and track) and at least one student who could be classified as a serious but recreational, non-competitive athlete. While the project group would be the first to describe this level of usability testing as limited, they nevertheless felt that the feedback they received from their test group helped them identify design problems that they could correct before presenting to the class for project assessment.

Blitz: Portals—Vortals—Opinions

Portals on the Web serve as gateways to a variety of information and entertainment links according to the preferences set by a user—or by a portal service relying on various sorts of demographic profiles.

Vortals—a new term that may or may not find general acceptance—is simply a portal sliced vertically and more thinly than a general portal, a gateway to a more defined set of related links.

Blitz is a site created for lazy college students—students who want to buy stuff online without having to personally investigate numerous sites in search of what they want. The site organizes a limited selection of categories for online shopping (see figure 10.7). Clicking on a particular category brings up its page as shown in figure 10.8.

Figure 10.7
Blitz home page showing general categories for buying.

RATING	WEBSITE	COMMENTS
4.8	HomeRuns	Star Market to your door (more)
4.4	GongShee	Chinese snacks, foods and drinks without going to Chinatown... awww yeah (more)
4.3	Kozmo	Drinks, snacks, movies within the hour (more)
4.3	EthnicGrocer	Food from 15 different countries... international baby (more)
3.9	Peapod	Neat cart view feature, backed by stop and shop (more)
3.6	Greatfood	Want food for that hot date? Gourmet food - pricey! (more)
2.7	Food	Resturants that provide takeout and delivery (more)

Groceries, snacks, drinks to the door.

Figure 10.8
A sample Blitz page within a category showing the organization of information within that category.

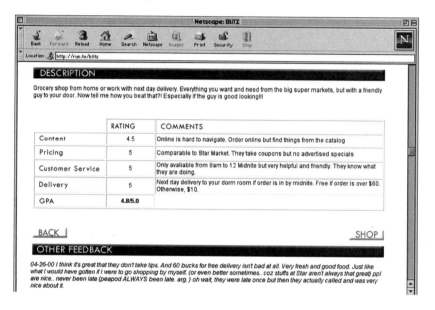

Figure 10.9
Blitz evaluation page with ratings, comments, and general feedback.

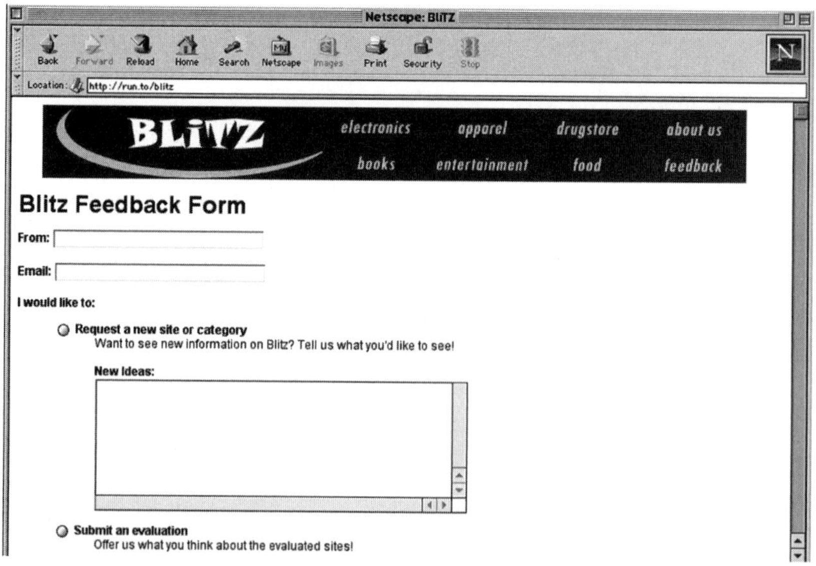

Figure 10.10
The Blitz feedback form.

The Blitz site adds value to this categorization by aggregating shoppers' evaluations of a particular site and assigning a "grade-point average" to each site as shown in figure 10.9. If a user is satisfied with the ratings presented on this page, he or she simply clicks on the SHOP link and is brought to the site to complete a transaction. The Blitz feedback form (figure 10.10) allows a user to suggest a new site to be added to the listings on Blitz; the form also allows a user to submit an opinion of a site currently listed on Blitz. Evaluations and general grade point averages are not sorted and calculated dynamically, so the site requires constant hands-on management and custodial service to keep information fresh.

Afterword

In *Mindstorms* Seymour Papert of the MIT Media Lab writes about the "protean ability" of the computer for simulation. Web sites amply demonstrate this power of computational technology to simulate (or even replace as some might argue) nondigital ways of interacting: brick-and-mortar stores, for example, turning into click-and-mortar online sites.

Web site design also illustrates another aspect of Papert's assertion. As we demonstrate in this guide, teaching the process of developing Web sites employs or simulates, to use Papert's word, a range of other nondigital processes as well: critical thought and analysis of objectives and needs, management and interpersonal skills, collaboration, peer review, and of course the "traditional" communication skills employed in writing and oral presentations.

A class in Web site design should not necessarily be viewed as purely computer-centric, as "being" only "digital." You have to be more than a skillful programmer to achieve success in cyberspace. We believe that the skills fostered in a class such as we present in this guide have a wide range of application beyond dotcom-dom. Our students not only are being educated in a particular kind of "invention," they also are developing skills that will be useful in many other fields, from mechanical engineering to teaching expository writing. Cyberspace, in other words, is a grand theater of educational experimentation, where individuals can work alone and in concert with others in preparation for future roles, whatever they may be.

Index

Accessibility
  ALT attributes, 62
  and color, 48
  and frames, 46
  and JavaScript, 74
  and PDF, 66
  and sound, 69
  and tables, 45
  text-only browsers, 62
Audience, 26–32
  confusing client with, 32
  primary/secondary audiences, 26–29
  using focus groups to define (*see*
    Focus groups)

Bandwidth, 30–32, 50, 60, 66, 69, 71
Berners-Lee, Tim, 1
Blitz, 94–97
Boston Chinatown, 87–89

Cascading style sheets (CSS), 46, 74–75
Case studies, 87–97
CGI scripts, 50, 76–77
  and image maps, 58
  and security, 51, 52
Class design and curriculum, 1–16
  class structure, 3
  class Web site, 4–5, 13–16
  physical space, 4
  syllabus, 5, 6
Client representative, 19
Content developer, 19
Cookies, 77–78

Copyright and intellectual property, 53

Discussion systems (BBS), 79–80
Dithering, 61–62
Dynamic HTML (DHTML), 75–76

Encryption, 50–52
  certificates, 52
  Secure Sockets Layer (SSL) 51, 52
Extensible Markup Language (XML),
  79

Flash, 71
Flowchart. *See* Site map
Focus groups, 29–30, 81, 82

GIF, 56
  animated, 58–59
Graphic design, 37, 44–48, 55
  color, 48 (*see also* Web-safe color
    palette)
  grid, 44–46
  typography, 47–48, 62–63
Graphic designer, 20, 44

Hypertext, 1, 35, 66

Image maps, 58
Information architect, 19

Java, 50, 71, 77, 79
JavaScript, 59, 74
JPEG, 56–57

Maintenance, 39, 40, 46
Microsoft PowerPoint, 67
MP3. *See* Sound
Multimedia, 65–71. *See also* Sound;
    Video
    virtual reality (*see* Virtual Reality (3-D))
Multimedia designer, 20

Navigation, 37, 42, 44, 58

Papert, Seymour, 99
Planning a Web site, 23–40
    defining identity/key messages, 24–25
    metaphor, 25–26
    setting objectives, 23–24
Portable Document Format (PDF),
    66–67
    and accessibility (*see* Accessibility)
Portable Network Graphic (PNG), 57
Privacy, 52–53
    and cookies, 77, 79
Production, 20
Programmer/system administrator, 21
Programming for interactivity, 73–80
Project manager, 19
Proposals, 7–13
    alpha (initial) design, 7–8
    beta design, 10–13
    final presentation, 13
    oral presentation, 8–9
    written proposal, 9–10
QuickTime. *See* Video

RealAudio. *See* Sound
Reports. *See* Proposals

Security, 50–52
    passwords, 51
Server-side includes (SSI), 75
Shockwave, 71
Site map, 10, 11, 37, 42–44
Sound, 68–69
    file formats, 68
SweatStats, 90–94

Team-based Web design, 17–22
    team roles, 17–18, 19–21
    team size, 17
Technical designer, 20
Technology researcher, 19
Tester/focus group coordinator, 21
Testing and evaluating a Web site,
    81–86
    access logs, 83
    analysis, 86
    focus groups (*see* Focus groups)
    interviews, 81–82
    surveys, 85
    usability testing (*see* Usability testing)

Usability testing, 83–85
    card sorting, 85
    identifying observers, 83
    identifying users, 84
    in SweatStats class project, 94
    questions/tasks, 84–85
    talking protocol method, 83

Video, 69–71
    codec, 69
    file formats, 69–70
Virtual reality (3-D), 70–71

Web graphics, 55, 56, 57–60
    file formats, 55–57
    file size, 60–61
Web page publisher/editor, 21
Web-safe color palette, 48, 62
Web servers, 49–50
    back-end capabilities, 50
    hardware, 50
    planning, 49–50
    software, 50
Webmaster, 18
Writer, 19
Writing for the Web, 33–36

XML, 79